Author: One Exam Prep (1-877-804-3959)
www.1examprep.com

VISIT US HERE FOR EXCLUSIVE OFFERS

Unleashing the Power Of Digital Marketing For Your Contractor Business

- Company Branding
- Contractor Website
- Social Media Templates
- 1-on-1 Marketing Consultations
- Google Search Optimazation

WWW.154AGENCY.COM

TABLE OF CONTENTS

PRACTICE EXAMS

Florida Building Code 5
General Math 17
Determining Block for Wall 27
Purchasing Drywall 32
Drywall Math 38
Excavation and Hauling 48
Concrete Calculations 55
GC, BC, RC Math Test 66
Reading Blueprints 82
Contract Administration #1 86
Contract Administration #2 101
Contract Administration #3 116
Contract Administration #4 139
Project Management #1 156
Project Management #2 170
Project Management #3 184

Florida Building Codes, 2020
State General, Building, and Residential Contractors
Practice Exam

1. _____ would not require a building permit.

    A. Installing a reverse osmosis under sink water filter
    B. Replacing a kitchen sink
    C. Installing a portable air conditioner
    D. All of the above

2. The maximum rise for any ramp run, without an intervening landing, is _____.

    A. 30 inches
    B. 15 inches
    C. 12 inches
    D. Unlimited ramp run

3. When building in a public right away, a marquee or canopy which extends over the public right of way, such as a sidewalk, must have a minimum clearance of _____ feet, to the surface of the sidewalk.

    A. 10
    B. 9
    C. 8
    D. 7

4. Door openings shall provide a clear width of _____ inches minimum.

    A. 24
    B. 32
    C. 36
    D. 48

5. A property, used exclusively as a single family home, consisting of a basement and three stories of living space is governed by _____.

    A. The Florida Building Code, Residential only
    B. The Florida Building Code, Building only
    C. Both of the above
    D. Neither of the above

6. A building used as a carwash facility has an occupancy classification of _____ Occupancy.

    A. Assembly
    B. Mercantile
    C. Special
    D. Business

7. In a commercial building, showers used for other than safety reasons shall be equipped with flow control devices to limit the water discharge to a maximum of _____ gpm per shower head.

    A. 1.0
    B. 1.5
    C. 2.0
    D. 2.5

8. Exit passageways in a commercial building (occupant load more than 50) shall have a minimum width of _____ inches.

    A. 32
    B. 36
    C. 44
    D. None of the above

9. An access opening to an attic space must not be less than _____.

    A. 18" x 24"
    B. 24" x 36"
    C. 20" x 30"
    D. 20" x 24"

10. Mass common walls require an R-value of _____.

    A. 30
    B. 19
    C. 11
    D. 6

11. When constructing a masonry chimney located in the interior of the building or within the exterior wall of a building, a minimum airspace clearance of _____ inch(es) must be maintained with respect to any combustible to materials.

    A. 1
    B. 2
    C. 3
    D. 4

12. In order to resist fire spreading between townhouse units, separate exterior walls shall include a parapet not less than _____ inches above the roof line.

    A. 12
    B. 16
    C. 18
    D. 24

13. When an emergency repair is undertaken, in a property that has previously been issued a certificate of occupancy, such repair may be undertaken provided that the permit covering the work shall be applied for no later than _____.

    A. 24 hours after the repair is completed
    B. The next business day after the repair is completed
    C. The next working business day after the repair is begun
    D. 24 hours after the repair is begun

14. _____ may be added without requiring compliance with the light and ventilation requirements of the *Florida Building Code, Building*.

    A. Doors
    B. Windows
    C. Skylights
    D. None of the Above

15. When evaluating repairs and renovations of more than one category in an existing building, all related work permitted within a _____ month period shall be considered a single work project.

    A. 6
    B. 12
    C. 18
    D. 24

16. Which of the following is NOT true with respect to Chapter One of the *Florida Building Code, Building*?

    A. Under certain circumstances, construction work may proceed before a permit is issued
    B. Property owners may obtain a permit to remove asbestos in a single family home without formal asbestos training, provided certain conditions are followed
    C. Proof of compliance with Workers Compensation Law must be provided as part of the permit application process
    D. A properly licensed Architect or Engineer can provide structural inspections for municipal authorities under the "privatization" provision within the code

17. The minimum acceptable SEER rating for a $\leq$ 65,000 Btu/h central air conditioning system is _____.

    A. 11
    B. 12
    C. 13
    D. 14

18. All replacement doors shall be _____ inch(es) solid bonded wood core or approved equivalent, unless the existing frame will accommodate only a 1 3/8-inch door.

    A. 2
    B. 1 ¼
    C. 1 ½
    D. 1 ¾

19. In residential dwelling units, the seat height of water closets shall be permitted to be _____ inches minimum and _____ inches maximum above the finish floor, measured at the top of the seat.

    A. 16, 18
    B. 16, 20
    C. 17, 19
    D. 15, 19

20. An access opening to an attic space for detached one- and two-family and multiple single-family dwellings not more than three stories above grade in height must not be less than _____.

    A. 22" x 30"
    B. 18" x 24"
    C. 24" x 36"
    D. 20" x 24"

Please see Answer Key on the following page*

ABC 09/20/2021

Florida Building Codes, 2020
State General, Building, and Residential Contractors
Practice Exam
Answer Key

	Answer	Reference	Section #
1.	C	Building	105.2
2.	A	Building	1012.4
3.	C	Building	3202.2
4.	B	Accessibility	404.2.3
		Building	1010.1.1
5.	A	Building	101.2, Exception 1
6.	D	Building	304.1
7.	D	Energy Conservation	C404.12.1
8.	C	Building	1024.2
9.	C	Building	1209.2
10.	D	Energy Conservation	R402.2.14
11.	B	Building	2113.19
12.	C	Building	706.4.1.1 (1)
13.	C	Building	105.2.1
14.	B	Existing Building	801.3(1)
15.	B	Building	Appendix J, AJ101.3
16.	D	Building	105.2.1, 105.3.6, 105.3.5
17.	C	Energy Conservation	Table C403.2.3(1)
18.	D	Existing Building	805.5.1
19.	C	Accessibility	604.4
20.	A	Residential	R807.1

1 Exam Prep
2017 Florida Building Codes
Practice Exam
(State General, Building, and Residential Contractors)

1. Which of the following activities would NOT require a building permit?

    A. Installing a reverse osmosis under sink water filter
    B. Replacing a kitchen sink
    C. Installing a portable air conditioner
    D. All of the above

2. According to *The Florida Building Code*, the maximum rise for any ramp run (without an intervening landing) is:

    A. 30"
    B. 15"
    C. 12"
    D. Unlimited ramp run

3. When building in a public right away, a marquee or canopy which extends over the public right of way, such as a sidewalk, must have a minimum clearance of _____feet, to the surface of the sidewalk.

    A. 10
    B. 9
    C. 8
    D. 7

4. Door openings shall provide a clear width of _____ inches minimum?

    A. 24
    B. 32
    C. 36
    D. 48

5. A property, used exclusively as a single family home, consisting of a basement and three stories of living space is governed by:

   A. The Florida Building Code. Residential only
   B. The Florida Building Code, Building only
   C. Both of the above
   D. Neither of the above

6. A building used as a carwash facility has an occupancy classification of:

   A. Assembly Occupancy
   B. Mercantile Occupancy
   C. Special Occupancy
   D. Business Occupancy

7. In a commercial building, showers used for other than safety reasons shall be equipped with flow control devices to limit the water discharge to a maximum of _____ gallons per minute per shower head.

   A. 1.0 gpm
   B. 1.5 gpm
   C. 2.0 gpm
   D. 2.5 gpm

8. Exit passageways in a commercial building (occupant load more than 50) shall have a minimum width of _____ inches.

   A. 32
   B. 36
   C. 44
   D. None of the above

9. Notches at the ends of structural floor members such as solid lumber joists shall not exceed _____ the depth of the member. Holes shall be bored not within _____ of the top or bottom of the member or to any other hole not located in the member.

   A. 1/8 depth : 1 inch
   B. 1/4 depth: 2 inch
   C. 1/8 depth; 2 inch
   D. ¼ depth; 1 inch

10. Mass common walls require an R-value of _____ ?

    A. 30
    B. 19
    C. 11
    D. 6

11. When constructing a masonry chimney located in the interior of the building or within the exterior wall of a building, a minimum airspace clearance of _____must be maintained with respect to ANY combustible to materials.

    A. 1"
    B. 2"
    C. 3"
    D. 4"

12. In order to resist fire spreading between townhouse units, separate exterior walls shall include a parapet not less than _____above the roof line.

    A. 12"
    B. 16"
    C. 18"
    D. 24"

13. When an emergency repair is undertaken, in a property that has previously been issued a certificate of occupancy, such repair may be undertaken provided that the permit covering the work shall be applied for no later than:

    A. 24 hours after the repair is completed
    B. The next business day after the repair is completed
    C. The next working business day after the repair is begun
    D. 24 hours after the repair is begun

14. _____ may be added without requiring compliance with the light and ventilation requirements of the Florida Building Code, Building.

    A. Doors
    B. Windows
    C. Skylights
    D. None of the Above

5. When evaluating repairs and renovations of more than one category in an existing building, all related work permitted within a _____ month period shall be considered a single work project.

    A. 6
    B. 12
    C. 18
    D. 24

16. Which of the following is NOT true with respect to Chapter One of the *Florida Building Code, Building*?

    A. Under certain circumstances, construction work may proceed before a permit is issued
    B. Property owners may obtain a permit to remove asbestos in a single family home without formal asbestos training, provided certain conditions are followed
    C. Proof of compliance with Workers Compensation Law must be provided as part of the permit application process
    D. A properly licensed Architect or Engineer can provide structural inspections for municipal authorities under the "privatization" provision within the code

17. The minimum acceptable SEER rating for a $\leq 65,000$ Btu/h central air conditioning system is _____.

    A. 11
    B. 12
    C. 13
    D. 14

18. All replacement doors shall be _____ inch solid bonded wood core or approved equivalent, unless the existing frame will accommodate only a 1 3/8-inch door.

    A. 2
    B. 1 ¼
    C. 1 ½
    D. 1 ¾

19. In residential dwelling units, the seat height of water closets shall be permitted to be _____ inches minimum and _____ inches maximum above the finish floor, measured at the top of the seat.

    A. 16, 18
    B. 16, 20
    C. 17, 19
    D. 15, 19

20. An access opening to an attic space for detached one- and two-family and multiple single-family dwellings not more than three stories above grade in height must not be less than _____.

     A. 22" x 30"
     B. 18" x 24"
     C. 24" x 36"
     D. 20" x 24"

21. An access opening to an attic space must not be less than _____.

     A. 18" x 24"
     B. 24" x 36"
     C. 20" x 30"
     D. 20" x 24"

Please scroll down to see answer key on page 6

1 Exam Prep
Florida Building Codes, 2017
Answers

1. C	Building	105.2	
2. A	Building	1012.4	
3. C	Building	3202.2	
4. B	Accessibility	404.2.3	
	and Building	1010.1.1	
5. A	Building	101.2 Exception: 1	
6. D	Building	304.1	
7. D	Energy Conservation	C404.12.1	
8. C	Building	1024.2	
9. B	Residential	R502.8.1	
10. D	Energy Conservation	R402.2.14	
11. B	Building	2113.19	
12. C	Building	706.4.1.1 (1)	
13. C	Building	105.2.1	
14. B	Existing Building	801.3	
15. B	Building	Appendix J, AJ101.3	
16. D	Building	105.2.1, 105.3.6, 105.3.5	
17. C	Energy Conservation	Table C403.2.3(1)	
18. D	Existing Building	805.5.1	
19. C	Accessibility	604.4	
20. A	Residential	R807.1	
21. C	Building	1209.2	

Books NOT Allowed into the Exam

1. Walker's Building Estimator's Reference - Information to Know for GC/BC/RC Exam
2. Walker's Building Estimator's Reference, 32nd Edition
3. Walker's Building Estimator's Reference, 31st Edition
4. Builders Guide to Accounting
5. Design and Control of Concrete Mixtures, 17th Ed.
6. Design and Control of Concrete Mixtures, 16th Ed.
7. Placing Reinforcing Bars
8. Application and Finishing of Gypsum Panel Products, GA-216, 2018
9. Application and Finishing of Gypsum Panel Products, GA-216 Questions, 2016 - 1
10. Application and Finishing of Gypsum Panel Products, GA-216 Questions, 2016 - 2

GENERAL MATH FOR PASSING

Your math and problem solving skills will be a key element in achieving a passing score on your exam. It will be necessary to brush up on your math and problem solving skills. To help you, *1 Exam Prep* has prepared this math review. Work through the examples on the following pages to gain the math experience you will need. The purpose of this unit is to learn or relearn general math rules and skills you need. Do not skip this unit.

Construction math deals mostly with areas, volumes, and time calculations. The purpose of this unit is to give you an overview of general math; the specific math skills for each facet of the trade will be covered in the section dealing with that facet.

Note: Your specific trade math is covered in its own unit.

THE ROSE OF PROBLEM SOLVING

R - Read for understanding
O - Organize the information given:

Setting the problem up: When you set up a problem (get ready to solve it), remember the following steps, and take them one at a time:

- Always write the formula you will be using before doing anything else.
- Write down the values for each letter in the formula.
- Show each step of your work
- Write in a logical sequence.
- Always label your answer in the units.
- Keep your work neat.
- Avoid division when you can multiply.
- Avoid working with large numbers

S - Solve the problem

E - Evaluate the answers (Does it look right? Remember, matching an answer does not mean it's right.)

ROUNDING DECIMALS

How many places should you carry an answer beyond the decimal point? The rule of thumb is three (3) places unless you see that one more place will make your answer even. When you round your answer, the rule is as follows:

- If the number is below 5, round down.
- If the number is 5 or more, add one to the number to the left.

For example, 1.743 rounded to two decimal places would be 1.74, but 1.747 rounded to 2 places would be 1.75

DO NOT ROUND ANY NUMBERS UNTIL YOU HAVE THE FINAL ANSWER.

PARENTHESIS AND BRACKETS

In the previous example, we used the expression (3' x 3') + (4' x 4'). What do the parentheses mean? They simply mean to do whatever is inside them first. In other words, we are to take 3 times 3 (9) and add it to 4 times 4 (16). If we ignored the parentheses, we would get 3 x 3 + 4 x 4 = 52 which is very different from 25.

The rule for working complex math problems is as follows. Use the acronym PEMDAS - Please Excuse My Dear Aunt Sally to help you remember

1st   Parentheses - groupings are always done from the innermost set outward – inside to outside

2nd   Exponents - Applying an exponent is different than just multiplying - 2^3 means 2 x 2 x 2 = 8

3rd   Multiply and Divide - These operations are done in the order from left to right. They are done together because they have the same importance.

4th   Add and Subtract - Here again, they are done together because they have the same importance. These are done in the order left to right.

For example, 5 x 3 + 4 = 19. But if the problem calls for us to add 3 and 4 first, then multiply by 5, we would write 5 x (3 + 4). The answer is 35, because 3 + 4 = 7 and 5 x 7 = 35.

Sometimes, brackets are used to surround parentheses. If this happens, you do whatever is inside the parentheses first, then the brackets from left to right, then everything else from left to right. 7 x [(6 + 4) + (8 -3)] = 105, because 6 + 4 = 10, 8 - 3 = 5, 10 + 5 = 15, and 7 x 15 = 105. Follow this through, and make sure you understand. If you ignore the parentheses and brackets, you get 7 x 6 + 4 + 8 - 3 = 51, which is the wrong answer. Pay attention to the parentheses and brackets, and you'll be OK.

SYMBOLS

Math is a system of numbers, signs, and symbols, each of which has a unique and consistent meaning that you must understand before proceeding further. Formulas are stated using letters to represent numbers which you must substitute into the formulas to solve them. In solving problems, first write the formula (with the letters), then replace any letters you already know with their values.

Here are some examples of the way formulas might be stated. In the following examples, A is always 9" and B is always 6". C is the unknown quantity we will be solving for:

ADDITION:	C = A + B	C = 9" + 6"	C = 15"
SUBTRACTION:	C = A - B	C = 9" - 6"	C = 3"
MULTIPLICATION:	C = A x B	C = 9"x 6"	C = 54 square inches
	C = A • B	C = 9" x 6"	C = 54 square inches
	C = AB	C = 9" x 6"	C = 54 square inches

Note the usage in the multiplication problems above. All of the above forms are seen in formulas, with "x" being by far the most common. The dot (•) is seldom seen, but you need to know what it means when it happens. Sometimes the sign is omitted altogether.

DIVISION:	C = A ÷ B	C = 9" ÷ 6"	C = 1.5"
	$C = \dfrac{A}{B}$	$C = \dfrac{9}{6}$	C = 1.5"
	$C = B\overline{)A}$	$C = 6\overline{)9}$	C = 1.5"

All three signs for division are acceptable; you just have to know what they mean.

A ÷ B   Means A divided by B $\frac{A}{B}$ Means A divided by B

B$\overline{)A}$ Means B divided into A, or A divided by B

EXPONENTS

When a number is multiplied by itself a certain number of times, as in 4 x 4, an exponent is often used 4 x 4 can be abbreviated as 4^2 . This is read as "four squared" or "four to the second power. The exponent is the little number above and to the right of the number and tells you how many times the number is being multiplied by itself.

For example: 5^3= 5 x 5 x 5 = 125 and 6^4 is the same as writing 6 x 6 x 6 x 6 = 1296. Why would anyone want to write out 8 x 8 x 8 x 8 x 8 x 8 x 8 x 8 x 8 x 8 when they could just write 8^{10}? They wouldn't! That's why we have exponents.

Exponents are also used to abbreviate certain measurements. Square feet (Sq. ft.) is often abbreviated ft^2. As we will see, areas are always measured in square units, so this shorthand will come in very handy.

Volumes are measured in cubic units. A number to, the third power is often called the "cube" of that number. So in^3, ft^3, and yd^3 are common abbreviations for cubic inches, cubic feet, and cubic yards. For example, how many cubic feet are in a cubic yard? yd3 = 3 ft/yd x 3 ft/yd x 3 ft/yd = 27 ft^3/yd^3.

SQUARE ROOTS

Square roots are related to exponents. The square of 4 is 16; therefore the square root of 16 is 4. Another way to say this is that the square root of any number "A" is the number that you have to multiply by itself to get "A". If we call the square root "B", we would write "the square root of A is B" this way: B$\sqrt{A}$ The symbol is called the "square root sign."

Squares and square roots are frequently used in the trades. Often, we need to find the length of the third side of a right triangle. As long: we know that one of the angles is 90°, and we know the length of the two sides that form that angle, we can find the length of the third side.

Suppose we need to know the length of side C in the following triangle. This triangle could represent the corner of a lot, the corner of a house, or anything else. Here is the triangle:

Now, a very smart Greek guy was sitting around thinking about triangles one day and figured out a way to find the length of the unknown side. His name was Pythagorean, and his way of figuring out the length of that side is called the Pythagorean Theorem. It still works today, 3,000 years later. In fact, it's the only easy way to find the length of that side. Here it is $C = \sqrt{a^2 + b^2}$

A and B are the sides that we know about, and C is the one we need to know. Let's plug in the values for the triangle that we know about, and solve for C.

19

$$C = \sqrt{a^2 + b^2} \qquad C = \sqrt{(3 \times 3) + (4 \times 4)} \qquad C = \sqrt{9 + 16} \qquad C = \sqrt{25} \qquad C = 5$$

Reverse to find A or B $\qquad A = \sqrt{C^2 + B^2} \qquad A = \sqrt{5^2 + 4^2} \qquad A = \sqrt{(5 \times 5) - (3 \times 3)}$

$$A = \sqrt{25 - 9} \qquad A = \sqrt{16} \qquad A = 4$$

THE CALCULATOR

The calculator pictured is an example of a good basic model which you can purchase for around $5.00 in discount stores. In addition to the standard keys (+, x, and ÷), it has a square root key (1) and a percent key (%). When buying a calculator to use during the exam, make sure that it has square root and percent keys. Memory is important to have on a calculator. It can help you store values while you are working on something else. There are three memory buttons on the above calculator. The M+ button adds the number in the display to the number in memory and the - button subtracts the number in the display from the number in the memory. The MRC button recalls the contents of memory to the display. Also make sure that the calculator you take to the exam is not too fancy Besides the fact that it may be difficult to find what you are looking for amid a maze of tiny little buttons, so-called "contractor's calculators" that have conversion formulas and programmable calculators are prohibited. You don't want to spend all of this time and money just to be kicked out of the exam because of your calculator.

Many calculators have two clear buttons, CE and C. The CE button clears the last number you entered. This can be handy; it keeps you from having to start all over again if you accidentally hit a wrong number. The C key wipes the whole mess out, so you can start over When using a calculator, you generally input the information just as you read it on the page. For example, if you saw this:

5+ 4 =? You would enter: | 5 | | + | | 4 | | = |

On your calculator, the answer **9** would be displayed on the screen.

Some calculations require a little different approach. If you want to take the square root of a number, you hit the number, then the square root key. To find the square root of 9, enter:

| 9 | | √ | | = | The answer is 3.

The percent key is a bit tricky to get used to, but once you understand it, it becomes one of your best friends. Let's say you are estimating the cost of materials which you are going to pay 7% sales tax on. What is the total material cost if the cost before taxes is 10,000? Here's what you would do:

| 1 | | 0 | | 0 | | 0 | | 0 | | + | | 7 | | % | The answer would be **$10,700.**

FRACTIONS

A fraction is some part of a whole. The word fraction comes from the Latin root fract-, which means "to break."When something is divided into two or more equal parts, those parts are called fractions.

Suppose you own and operate a pie shop. You sell three different kinds of pie: apple, key lime, and pecan. You sell your pie by the slice or by the whole pie. Apple pie costs $4.00; key lime costs $5.00; and pecan costs $6.00. The prices are for whole pies only. You cut your apple and key lime pies into 6 slices, and your pecan pie into 8, because pecans are more expensive. Here's what they look like:

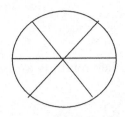 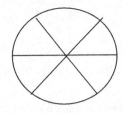 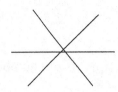

| **APPLE** | **KEY LIME** | **PECAN** |

So, you're sitting there one day, and a customer walks in. He asks you for a piece of apple pie. What do you charge him?

Since apple pie is cut into six pieces, the price per slice would be: $4.00 ÷ 6 = $0.67. Note that we rounded off 0.666 to 0.67. If the customer wanted 2 slices of apple pie the charge would have been 2 x 0.666 = $1.33, not 2 x 0.67 = $1.34. This is why you should not round off numbers until the end of the calculation.

The next customer wants 2 slices of key lime pie and 1 slice of apple pie. The price per slice of key lime pie is $5.00 ÷ 6 = $0.833. So you would charge him (2 x 0.833) + 0.67 = $2.34.

You seem to be having a good day, so you go in the back and bake more pies. The next customer walks in and asks for two slices of apple, three slices of key lime, and four slices of pecan. In the following formulas, "a" stands for the price of the apple, "k" for the key lime, and "p" for the pecan. Here are the formulas:

a = 2 x ($4.00 ÷ 6) = $1.33   **k = 3 x ($5.00 ÷ 6) = $2.50**   **p = 4 x ($6.00 ÷ 8) = $3.00**

Total Price = a + k + p = 1.33 + 2.50 + 3.00 = $ 6.83:

By now you are really tired of selling pie and decide to learn more about fractions.

TYPES OF FRACTIONS

There are three basic types of fractions, proper, improper, and mixed. EXAMPLES:

Proper: $\dfrac{1}{3}$ **Improper:** $\dfrac{3}{2}$ **Mixed:** $3\dfrac{1}{3}$

When the numerator of a fraction is smaller than the denominator, the fraction is proper. Proper fractions have a value of less than one. If the numerator is greater than the denominator, the fraction is said to be improper. When the numerator denominator are equal, the value of the fraction is ONE. (Neither proper nor improper) Remember that last sentence, it becomes very important later.

Mixed fractions have a whole number part and a fractional part. The fraction is proper. A mixed number can always be converted to an improper fraction by multiplying the whole number by the denominator, adding the numerator, and putting the result over the denominator:

Improper fractions can be converted to mixed numbers by dividing the numerator by the denominator, taking the result as the whole number, and the remainder as the numerator:

17/3 is an improper fraction. 3 goes into 17 five times with two left over. 2 is the remainder:

$$\frac{17}{3} = 5\frac{2}{3}$$

MULTIPLYING FRACTIONS

To multiply two fractions, multiply the numerators and denominators, then reduce:

$$\frac{1}{2} \times \frac{2}{3} \times \frac{2}{6} = \frac{1}{9}$$

$$\frac{1}{4} \times \frac{1}{2} = \frac{1}{8}$$

To multiply mixed numbers, first convert them to improper fractions, and then multiply as usual:

$$3\frac{1}{2} \times 2\frac{1}{3} = \frac{(3 \times 2)+1}{2} \times \frac{(2 \times 3)=1}{3} = \frac{7}{2} \times \frac{7}{3} = \frac{49}{6} = 8\frac{1}{6}$$

ADDING AND SUBTRACTING FRACTIONS

Adding and subtracting fractions is easy, provided the denominators are the same. Since they hardly ever are, you must first find a common denominator. You obtain this number by finding a number that all of the denominators will go into evenly. Once you find this number, you multiply the numerator of the fractions by the number of times each denominator goes into the common denominator. A picture is worth a thousand words:

$$\frac{1}{2} + \frac{2}{3}$$

The common denominator is 6, since both 2 and 3 go into 6 evenly.

$$\frac{?}{6} + \frac{?}{6}$$

To find the new numerators, we multiply each old numerator by the number of times its denominator goes into 6. 2 goes into 6 three times, and 3x1 = 3, so the first fraction is . The second fraction is , since 3 goes into 6 two times, and 2x2 = 4. Once you have the two new fractions, just add the numerators and keep the same denominator. Reduce, if necessary.

$$\frac{3}{6} + \frac{4}{6} = \frac{7}{6} = 1\frac{1}{6}$$

To subtract fractions, use the same procedure, subtracting the numerators instead of adding them:

$$\frac{2}{3} - \frac{1}{2} = \frac{4}{6} - \frac{3}{6} = \frac{1}{6}$$

CONVERTING FRACTIONS TO DECIMALS

To convert a fraction to a decimal, you will divide the part by the whole. Remember, a decimal is also a percent. Example:

$$.25 = \frac{25}{100} \qquad 25 \div 100 = 25\%$$

Examples: Part ÷ Whole

$$\frac{6"}{12"} = 6" \div 12" = .5' \qquad .5 \times 100 = 50\% \text{ of a foot}$$

$$\frac{30\ min.}{60\ min.} = 30\ min \div 60\ min. = .5\ hr.$$

$$\frac{1}{2}" = 1 \div 2 = .5$$

CONVERTING DECIMALS TO FRACTIONS OR WHOLE NUMBERS

Remember, to get the decimal you divide the part by the whole. Now we will multiply the decimal part times the whole to get the fraction or whole number. For example:

.5" x 12" = 6"

.5 hr, x 60 min. = 30 min.

.5 of an inch x 16 = 8 inches

.5 of an inch x 4 = 2 inches

$$\frac{0.75"}{1} \quad X \quad \frac{16"}{16} = \frac{12"}{16} = \frac{3"}{4}$$

What you are doing is multiplying the "parts times the whole." This is an extremely important concept because when you are dealing with rulers, you are dealing with fractions, but when you are dealing with calculators, you are dealing with decimals. Being able to convert between one and the other is very important. Let's do another one. What is 0.25' expressed as a fraction?

$$\frac{0.25'}{1} \quad X \quad \frac{12}{12} = \frac{3}{12} = \frac{1}{4} = 3"$$

Note: With inches, any number can be a whole inch: 16/16, 8/8, 4/4, etc. B.T.E.S. uses a 16th because this is the smallest part of a construction ruler.

Here are some examples:

6" is what % of a whole foot?
6" is 6 parts of a foot or 12" (remember the whole needs to be in the same unit.)
6" ÷ 12" = .5 or 50% of a foot
15 min. is what % of an hour?
15 min. ÷ 60 min. = 25%

There are a few decimals that you should just know. Stick them in your mind. The most common are:

0.0625" = 1/16"	0.3125" = 5/16"	0.565" = 9/16	0.1875" = 3/16"
0.125" = 1/8"	0.375" = 3/8"	0.625" = 5/8"	0.875" = 7/8"
0.1875" = 3/16"	0.4375" = 7/16"	0.6875" = 11/16"	0.9375" = 15/16"
0.25" = 1/4"	0.5" = 1/2"	0.75" = 3/4"	1 " = 1"

PERCENTAGES

A percentage is like a fraction or decimal. It is part of the whole. The word percent comes from two Latin words: per, meaning for and centum meaning one-hundred. A percent, therefore, is a part of 100.

Let's suppose that we have a very large pizza that is cut into 100 equal pieces. If you eat 10 pieces of this pizza, you have eaten 10 percent (10%) of the pizza. If your neighbor, Joe, eats 43 pieces, not only is he a pig, but he has eaten 43% of the pizza. After you and Joe get through, 53% of the pizza is gone, and 47% is left. Why? Because 100 — 53 = 47. *Remember, percentages always relate to 100.*

It is often easier to multiply a number by a percentage rather than by a fraction and it is always easier than dividing. In this section, we will show you a couple of little tricks to make your fractions and division easier. But first, let's learn how to convert a fraction to a percentage.

CONVERTING FRACTIONS TO PERCENT OR DECIMAL

Remember, a fraction and a percent are the same. It is how they are expressed or put on paper that is different. For example: With money, would you say you had 50% of a dollar or simply say a half dollar or 50 cents. Or was the price 50% lower or 1/2 as much. Each have their own place in the scheme of things. Percent will always be found by dividing a part of a whole by the whole in the same unit. Example: 50 cents is 50 parts

23

of thewhole 100 cents. Percent = 50 ÷ 100 = .50 x 100 = 50%. With todays calculator, % = 50 ÷ 100. Hit the % key and decimal is moved. 50. or 50%. There are two steps to converting a fraction to a percent.

      1. Divide the fraction out on your calculator.
      2. Multiply the result by 100.

Here are some examples: **1/2 = 1 ÷ 2 = 0.50 and .5 x 100 = 50%**
                                3/5 = 3 ÷ 5 = 0.6 and 0.6 x 100 = 60%
                                5/8 = 5 8 = 0.625 and 0.625 x 100 = 62.5%

In summary, to get a percent, the part of something is divided by the whole something. So asking what 1/2 of something is the same as asking what 50% of something is 60% of a gallon is the same as 3/5ths of a gallon. 5/8 of an inch is 62.5% of an inch.

Here are some problems using percentages:

1. A job costing $5,000.00 is figured to have 12% overhead. What is the total cost of the job?

| 5 | 0 | 0 | 0 | | + | | 1 | 2 | | % |

The calculator reads **5600,** *so the cost of the job is $5,600.00*

2. If sales tax is 7%, what is the cost, including tax, of an item with a price of $34.50?

| 3 | 4 | . | 5 | 0 | | + | | 7 | | % |

The calculator reads **36.915.** *We round to the nearest cent, and get* **$36.92.**

3. If a job requires 200 pounds of lead, and you figure on 6% waste, what will be the total job need in pounds of lead ?

| 2 | 0 | 0 | | + | | 6 | | % |

The calculator reads **212,** *so you will need* **212** *lbs of lead.*

4. You get a deal on a quantity of lead 10% less than the going rate, which is $150 for that quantity. What will you pay?

| 1 | 5 | 0 | | - | | 1 | 0 |

You will be paying **$135.**

5. Joe Invested $20,000 and Bill invested $30,000. What percent does Joe own? What is the relationship or part and whole.

Solution: It is Joe's part of the total investment, so 20,000 is to 50,000; (is to) is a key phrase for division: 20 000 ÷ 50 000 = 40%.

GENERAL MATH TEST QUESTIONS

Adding fractions:

1. $\frac{2}{4} + \frac{12}{16}$

2. $\frac{3}{16} + \frac{7}{8} + \frac{3}{64}$

3. $\frac{3}{5} + \frac{3}{4}$

Subtracting fractions:

4. $\frac{3}{8} - \frac{3}{16}$

5. $\frac{4}{5} - \frac{1}{2}$

6. $\frac{1}{4} - \frac{1}{16}$

Converting fractions to decimals:

7. $\frac{3}{8}$

8. $\frac{1}{16}$

9. $\frac{2}{5}$

Converting inches into decimals of a foot:

10. 3"

11. $1\frac{1}{2}$"

12. 8"

Converting decimal feet to inches and fractions of an inch:

13. .25'

14. .125'

15. .375'

Converting decimal inches to a fraction of an inch:

16. .25"

17. .60 to the nearest 1/8th

18. .80 to the nearest 1/16th

Percentages:

19. 6" is what % of a yard?

20. 2' is what % of a yard?

21. 20 minutes is what % of an hour?

22. 12" of fall in a 100', is what % per 100.

Converting decimals to fractions or wholes:

23. .25"

24. .25'

25. .25 hour

Numbers and Powers:

26. 4^2 27. $3'^2$ 28. $3'^3$

Square Roots:

29. $\sqrt{25}$ 30. $\sqrt{144}$ 31. $\sqrt{289}$

ANSWERS TO GENERAL MATH TEST

1. $1\frac{1}{4}$ 2. $1\frac{7}{64}$ 3. $1\frac{7}{20}$

4. $\frac{3}{16}$ 5. $\frac{3}{10}$ 6. $\frac{3}{16}$

7. .375   8. .0625   9. .400

10. .25'   11. .125'   2. .666'

13. 3"   14. 1 ½"   15. 4 ½"

16. $\frac{4}{16}$"or $\frac{1}{4}$"   17. $\frac{5}{8}$"   18. $\frac{13}{16}$"

19. 16.66%   20. 66.66%   21. 33.33%   22. 1%

23. $\frac{4}{16}$"or $\frac{1}{4}$"   24. 3"   25. 15 minutes

26. 16   27. 9'   28. 27'

29. 5   30. 12   31. 17

How to Determine the Number of Blocks to Build a Wall
Questions and Answers

1. If you are building a wall using 8x8x16 concrete block, and the wall is 40 feet long and 6 feet high. How many blocks will you need to build the wall?

    A. 30
    B. 270
    C. 688
    D. 1,920

2. If you are building a wall using 12x12x16 concrete block, and the wall is 20 feet long and 6 feet high. How many blocks will you need to build the wall?

    A. 1920
    B. 1440
    C. 900
    D. 90

3. If you are building a wall using 6x6x12 concrete block, and the wall is 25 feet long and 10 feet high. How many blocks will you need to build the wall?

    A. 50
    B. 500
    C. 1500
    D. 3000

4. If you are building a wall using 8x8x16 concrete block, and the wall is 100 feet long and 6 feet high. How many blocks will you need to build the wall?

    A. 67
    B. 75
    C. 675
    D. 4800

5. If you are building a wall using 12x12x12 concrete block, and the wall is 18 feet long and 6 feet high. How many blocks will you need to build the wall?

    A. 1920 blocks
    B. 1080 blocks
    C. 108 blocks
    D. 90 blocks

6. If you are building a wall using 8x8x16 concrete block, and the wall is 40 feet long and 6 feet high. How many blocks will you need to build the wall?

    A. 70
    B. 270
    C. 1,920
    D. 2,700

7. If you are building a wall using 6x6x12 concrete block, and the wall is 36 feet long and 8 feet high. How many blocks will you need to build the wall?

    A. 3456
    B. 1,728
    C. 576
    D. None of the above

8. If you are building a wall using 8w x4h x 16lng concrete block, and the wall is 12 feet long and 6 feet high. How many blocks will you need to build the wall?

    A. 576
    B. 288
    C. 162
    D. 152

9. If you are building a wall using 8x8x16 concrete block, and the wall is 60 feet long and 4 feet high. How many blocks will you need to build the wall?

    A. 70
    B. 270
    C. 1,920
    D. 2,700

10. If you are building a wall using 10w x 9h x 15lng concrete block, and the wall is 50 feet long and 12 feet high. How many blocks will you need to build the wall?

    A. 5400
    B. 640
    C. 540
    D. None of the above

Please see Answer Key on the following page

ABC 09/20/2021

How to Determine the Number of Blocks to Build a Wall
Questions and Answers
Answer Key

Answer	**Solution:**

1. B

Convert 40 feet into inches:
40 feet x 12 = 480 inches
480 inches divided by 16 inches length = 30 blocks long

Convert 6 feet into inches:
6 x 12 = 72 inches
72 inches divided by 8 inches height= 9 blocks high

Multiply 9 blocks by 30 blocks = 270 blocks

2. D

Convert 20 feet into inches:
20 feet x 12 = 240 inches
240 inches divided by 16 inches length = 15 blocks long

Convert 6 feet into inches
6 x 12 = 72 inches
72 inches divided by 12 inches height = 6 blocks

Multiply 6 blocks by 15 blocks = 90 blocks high

3. B

Convert 25 feet into inches:
25 feet x 12 = 300 inches
300 inches divided by 12 inches length = 25 blocks long

Convert 10 feet into inches
10 x 12 = 120 inches
120 inches divided by 6 inches height = 20 blocks high

Multiply 25 blocks by 20 blocks = 500 blocks

4. C

Convert 100 feet into inches:
100 feet x 12 = 1,200 inches
1,200 inches divided by 16 inches length = 75 blocks long

Convert 6 feet into inches
6 x 12 = 72 inches
72 inches divided by 8 inches height = 9 blocks high

Multiply 75 blocks by 9 blocks = 675 blocks

Answer	**Solution:**

5. C

Convert 18 feet into inches:
18 feet x 12 = 216 inches
216 inches divided by 12 inches length = 18 blocks long

Convert 6 feet into inches
6 x 12 = 72 inches
72 inches divided by 12 inches height = 6 blocks high

Multiply 18 blocks by 6 blocks = 108 blocks

6. B

Convert 40 feet into inches:
40 feet x 12 = 480 inches
480 inches divided by 16 inches length = 30 blocks long

Convert 6 feet into inches
6 x 12 = 72 inches
72 inches divided by 8 inches height = 9 blocks high

Multiply 30 blocks by 9 blocks = 270 blocks

7. C

Convert 36 feet into inches:
36 feet x 12 = 432 inches
432 inches divided by 12 inches length = 36 blocks long

Convert 8 feet into inches
8 x 12 = 96 inches
96 inches divided by 6 inches height = 16 blocks high

Multiply 36 blocks by 16 blocks = 576 blocks

8. C

Convert 12 feet into inches:
12 feet x 12 = 144 inches
144 inches divided by 16 inches length = 9 blocks long

Convert 6 feet into inches
6 x 12 = 72 inches
72 inches divided by 4 inches height = 18 blocks high

Multiply 9 blocks by 18 blocks = 162 blocks

9. B

Convert 60 feet into inches:
60 feet x 12 = 720 inches
720 inches divided by 16 inches length = 45 blocks long

Convert 4 feet into inches
4 x 12 = 48 inches
48 inches divided by 8 inches height = 6 blocks high

Multiply 45 blocks by 6 blocks = 270 blocks

Answer	**Solution:**

10. B   Convert 50 feet into inches:
50 feet x 12 = 600 inches
600 inches divided by 15 inches long = 40 blocks long

Convert 12 feet into inches
12 x 12 = 144 inches
144 inches divided by 9 inches height = 16 blocks

Multiply 16 blocks by 40 blocks = 640 blocks

Purchasing Drywall
Practice Exam 1

Note: The best answer may be closest answer.

You are the subcontractor for a home that will need 83 sheets of drywall. Supplier # 1 Sells the drywall at $7.31 per sheet, plus 6% sales tax. Supplier # 2 is in another state, sells the same drywall for $6.95 per sheet and charges no sales tax. However, supplier # 2 does charge $.50 per sheet for delivery.

1. How much will be paid in state tax for supplier #1?

    A. $35.14
    B. $36.40
    C. $36.82
    D. $37.14

2. What is the total cost for drywall from Supplier #1?

    A. $528
    B. $609
    C. $627
    D. $640

3. What is the delivery cost only from Supplier #2?

    A. $41.50
    B. $46.00
    C. $52.50
    D. $83.00

4. What is the total cost for drywall from Supplier #2?

    A. $611
    B. $618
    C. $627
    D. $650

. Supplier #1, offers an 8% discount on the full total of all orders of over 50 sheets of drywall. Which of the
following is now true?

A. Supplier #2 is less expensive than Supplier #1
B. Supplier #1 has a final price of more than $600
C. Supplier #1 has a final price between $575 and $599
D. Supplier #1 has a final price between $550 and $574

****Please see Answer Key on the following page****

3/31/22

Purchasing Drywall
Practice Exam 1
Answer Key

	Answer	Solution

1.   B   83 sheets at \$7.31 per sheet: 83 x 7.31 = \$606.73
Tax is 6%: \$606.73 x .06 = \$36.40

2.   D   83 sheets at \$7.31 per sheet: 83 x 7.31 = \$606.73
Tax is 6%: \$606.73 x .06 = \$36.40
Total drywall cost from Supplier #1: \$606.73 + \$36.40 = \$643.13 (select closest answer)

3.   A   Drywall is delivery cost is 83 sheets at \$.50 per sheet: 83 x \$.50 = \$41.50

4.   B   Drywall cost is 83 sheets at \$6.95 per sheet: 83 x \$6.95 = \$576.85
Drywall is delivery cost is 83 sheets at \$.50 per sheet: 83 x \$.50 = \$41.50
Total drywall cost from Supplier #2: \$576.85 + \$41.50 = \$618.35 (select closest answer)

5.   C   83 sheets at \$7.31 per sheet: 83 x 7.31 = \$606.73
Tax is 6%: \$606.73 x .06 = \$36.40
Total drywall cost from Supplier #1: \$606.73 + \$36.40 = \$643.13 (select closest answer)
Discount of 8%: \$643.13 x .08 = \$51.45.
New total cost with volume discount from Supplier #1: \$643.13 - \$51.45 = \$591.68

Purchasing Drywall
Practice Exam 2

Note: The best answer may be closest answer.

You are the subcontractor for a home that will need 109 sheets of drywall. The supplier sells the drywall at $8.47 per sheet, plus a delivery charge of $.42 per sheet, plus 6% sales tax on the total, including delivery.

1. The delivery cost only from the supplier is _____.

    A. $56.33
    B. $45.78
    C. $59.62
    D. $41.30

2. The total cost for drywall delivered to the site is_____.

    A. $953
    B. $972
    C. $988
    D. $1,027

3. _____ will be paid in sales tax.

    A. $58.14
    B. $59.71
    C. $61.60
    D. $62.94

4. You just bought a truck. You will pick up the drywall, eliminating the delivery charge. The new total cost of the drywall, including tax is _____.

    A. $979
    B. $985
    C. $1,007
    D. $1,014

5. After buying the truck, you are informed that the supplier offers a 5% discount on the full total of all orders (before tax) of over 50 sheets of drywall for those who pick up their own orders. Your final cost of the drywall is now _____.

    A. $974.31
    B. $944.08
    C. $929.69
    D. $916.59

****Please see Answer Key on the following page****
ABC 09/21/2021

Purchasing Drywall
Practice Exam 2
Answer Key

Answer	Solution
B	109 sheets at \$.42 per sheet delivery: 109 x \$.42 = \$45.78
D	109 sheets at \$8.47 per sheet, plus \$.42 per sheet delivery: \$8.47 + \$.42 = \$8.89; 109 x \$8.89 = \$969.01 Tax is 6%: \$969.01 x .06 = \$58.14; \$969.01 + \$58.14 = \$1,027.15 (select closest answer)
A	109 sheets at \$8.47 per sheet, plus \$.42 per sheet delivery: \$8.47 + \$.42 = \$8.89; 109 x \$8.89 = \$969.01 Tax is 6%: \$969.01 x .06 = \$58.14
A	109 sheets at \$8.47 per sheet: \$109 x 8.47 = \$923.23 Tax is 6%: \$923.23 x .06 = \$55.39 \$923.23 + \$55.39 = \$978.62
C	109 sheets at \$8.47 per sheet: \$109 x 8.47 = \$923.23 Discount of 5%: \$923.23 x .05 = \$46.16. Total cost before tax with volume discount: \$923.23 - \$46.16 = \$877.07 Tax is 6%: \$877.07 x .06 = \$52.62 \$877.07 + \$52.62 = \$929.69

Drywall Math Calculations
Practice Test – 1

Please refer to diagram #1 as needed for the following ten questions.
Do not worry about doors, windows, closets, bathrooms, and halls. Assume the house is rectangular.
Best answer may be closest answer.

1. The total four wall perimeter for Bedroom (BR) 1 is _____ feet.

    A. 35
    B. 60
    C. 70
    D. 90

2. Excluding ceiling and floor, the four kitchen walls are a total of _____ square feet.

    A. 240
    B. 960
    C. 1224
    D. 1400

3. The total outside perimeter of this home is _____ feet

    A. 220
    B. 240
    C. 360
    D. 380

4. Sheets of drywall measure 4' x 12' x ½". _____ sheets will be needed for the kitchen.

    A. 20
    B. 22
    C. 24
    D. 18

5. In question 4, if drywall costs $8.27, per sheet, the drywall for the four kitchen walls will cost _____.

    A. $122.80
    B. $147.64
    C. $165.40
    D. $218.54

6. In the dining room, the total area of the four walls and the ceiling is _____ square feet.

   A. 1,660
   B. 1,892
   C. 2,020
   D. 2,282

7. In question 6, above, if the drywall is sold in 4' x 12' x ½" sheets, _____ sheets will be needed for the four walls and ceiling.

   A. 39
   B. 40
   C. 41
   D. 43

8. We see at the supply store that the drywall cost is up to $8.48 per sheet, and that they now must charge 6% sales tax on our drywall purchase. In questions 6 and 7, the total purchase price is _____.

   A. $122.80
   B. $147.64
   C. $165.40
   D. $386.52

9. The total amount of wall area for all three bedrooms (including ceilings but not floors) is between _____ square feet.

   A. 3,000 and 3,499
   B. 3,500 and 3,999
   C. 4,000 and 4,499
   D. 4,500 and 4,999

10. It is determined that the entire home will require 215 sheets of drywall.
    45 sheets of drywall are on hand from a previous job and will be used.
    The drywall contractor charges $2.85 per sheet to hang and finish each sheet.
    The supplier charges $7.45 per sheet of drywall, inclusive of sales tax.
    The total amount to be to the contractor by both the supplier and drywall contractor is _____.

    A. $1,880
    B. $1,900
    C. $2,126
    D. $2,280

DRYWALL CALCULATIONS - DIAGRAM #1

All Ceilings are 12'
Drawing not to scale

70'

30'		15'
Living Room 20'	Master Bedroom 20'	BR 1 20'
	25'	40'
20'		
Kitchen	Dining Room	BR 2
	35'	

****Please see Answer Key on the following page****

ABC 09/21/2021

Drywall Math Calculations
Practice Test – 1
Answer Key

Answer	Solution

1.   C

There are two walls 15' in length, and two walls 20' feet in length
15 + 15 + 20 + 20 = 70

2.   B

One kitchen wall is 20', as is the opposite wall
The other kitchen walls are also 20', because we see the short outside wall is 40' and living room is 20' of that 40'
So, four kitchen walls are each 20' x 12'.
20 x 12 = 240 square feet
240 x 4 = 960 square feet

3.   A

Rectangular home with length 70' and width 40'
70 + 70 + 40 + 40 = 220'

4.   A

From question 2, we know that total sf of kitchen is 960
Dry wall is 4' x 12' = 48 square feet per sheet
960 ÷ 48 = 20
So, 20 sheets are needed

5.   C

$8.27 x 20 (sheets needed) = $165.40

6.   C

The dining room is 35' long, 20' wide, and 12' high
Two of the walls are each: 35' x 12' = 420 sf
Two of the walls are each: 20' x 12' = 240 sf
Ceiling is 35' x 20' = 700 square feet
Total square footage of four walls and ceiling
420 + 420 + 240 + 240 + 700 = 2,020

7.   D

From question 6., we know that the dining room walls and ceiling total 2,020 sf
Drywall is 12' x 4'
12 x 4 = 48 square feet per sheet
2,020 ÷ 48 = 42.083 sheets
So, 43 sheets are needed
Note that we must have the extra sheet, even if only part of the sheet will be used

8.   D

$8.48 x 43 = $364.64 subtotal for drywall
6% sales tax is $364.64 x .06 = $21.88. $364.64 + $21.88 = $386.52

	Answer	**Solution**

9.   B

Bedroom 1 is 20' x 15' with a height of 12'
Two walls are 15' x 12' = 180 square feet each
Two walls are 20' x 12' = 240 square feet each
Ceiling is 15' x 20' = 300 square feet
180 + 180 + 240 + 240 + 300 = 1,140 total square feet for Bedroom 1

Bedroom 2 is identical to Bedroom 1, so BR 2 is also 1,140 square feet

Master Bedroom is 20' x 25' with a height of 12'
Two walls are 20' x 12' = 240 square feet each
Two walls are 25' x 12' = 300 square feet each
Ceiling is 20' x 25' = 500 square feet
240 + 240 + 300 + 300 + 500 = 1,580 total square feet for Master Bedroom

Three-bedroom total square feet is 1,140 + 1,140 + 1,580 = 3,860

10.   A

215 sheets of drywall to be hung
215 x $2.85 = $612.75
215 sheets needed, but already have 45
215 – 45 = 170
170 x $7.45 = $1,266.50
The total amount to be invoiced for this is $612.75 + $1,266.50 = $1,879.25

Drywall Math Calculations
Practice Test – 2

Please refer to Diagram # 2 as needed for the following ten questions.
Do not worry about doors, windows, closets, bathrooms, and halls. Assume the house is rectangular.
Best answer may be closest answer.

1. The total four wall perimeter for Bedroom (BR) 1 is _____ feet.

    A. 35
    B. 40
    C. 45
    D. 54

2. Excluding ceiling and floor, the four kitchen walls are a total of _____ square feet (sf).

    A. 1,128
    B. 1,206
    C. 1,434
    D. 1,877

3. The total square footage of this home is _____ square feet.

    A. 2,500
    B. 3,600
    C. 4,000
    D. 4,800

4. Sheets of drywall measure 4' x 12' x ½". _____ sheets will be needed for the kitchen.

    A. 21.5
    B. 21.25
    C. 22.75
    D. 23.5

5. In question 4, if drywall is sold by the sheet, and costs $8.17 per sheet, the drywall for the four kitchen walls will cost _____.

    A. $122
    B. $181
    C. $196
    D. $208

6. In the dining room, the total area of the four walls and the ceiling is _____ square feet.

    A. 1,500
    B. 1,530
    C. 1,684
    D. 1,930

7. In question 6, above, if the drywall is sold in 4' x 12' x ½" sheets, _____ sheets will be needed for the four walls and ceiling.

    A. 29
    B. 30
    C. 32
    D. 44

8. We see at the supply store that the drywall cost is up to $8.39 per sheet, and that they now must charge 6% sales tax on our drywall purchase. Per questions 6 and 7, the total purchase price of the drywall is _____.

    A. $207.96
    B. $242.18
    C. $268.48
    D. $284.59

9. The total amount of wall area for all three bedrooms (including ceilings but not floors) is between _____ square feet.

    A. 3,000 and 3,499
    B. 3,500 and 3,999
    C. 4,000 and 4,499
    D. 4,500 and 4,999

10. It is determined that the entire home will require 145 sheets of drywall.
    65 sheets of drywall are on hand from a previous job and will be used.
    The drywall contractor charges $2.95, inclusive of all taxes, per sheet to hang and finish each sheet.
    The supplier charges $.8.39 per sheet of drywall, plus 6% sales tax.
    The total amount to be invoiced to the contractor by both the supplier and drywall contractor is _____.

    A. $1,139
    B. $1,176
    C. $1,426
    D. $1,489

All Ceilings are 12'
Drawing not to scale

80'

30'	15'
Kitchen	
17'	BR 1 12'
	Master
	Bedroom
	BR 2 12'
15' Dining Room	50'
18' Living Room	Foyer Family Room
	26'
	34'

****Please see Answer Key on the following page****

ABC 09/21/2021

45

Drywall Math Calculations
Practice Test – 2
Answer Key

	Answer	**Solution**
1.	D	There are two walls 15' in length, and two walls 12' feet in length.
		15' + 15' + 12' + 12' = 54'

2.   A

One kitchen wall is 30' long x 12' high, as is the opposite wall
The other kitchen walls are each 17' long x 12'high.
30' x 12' = 360 square feet
360 x 2 walls:
360 square feet + 360 square feet = 720 square feet
17' x 12' = 204 square feet
204 x 2 walls
204 square feet + 204 square feet = 408 square feet
720 square feet + 408 square feet = 1,128 square feet total for kitchen walls w/out ceiling and floor

3.   C

Rectangular home with length 80' and width 50'
80' x 50' = 4,000 square feet

4.   D

From question 2, we know that total square feet of kitchen is 1,128 square feet.
Dry wall is 4' x 12' = 48 square feet per sheet
1,128 ÷ 48 = 23.5
23.5 sheets are needed.

5.   C

$8.17 x 24 (we need 23.5 but it's sold by the sheet) = $196.08

6.   B

Dining room is 30' long, 15' wide, and 12' high.
Two of the walls are each: 30' x 12' = 360 square feet
Two of the walls are each: 15' x 12' = 180 square feet
Ceiling is 30' x 15' = 450 square feet
Total square footage of four walls and ceiling:
360 + 360 + 180 + 180 + 450 = 1,530 square feet

7.   C

From question 6., we know that the dining room walls and ceiling total 1,530 square feet
Drywall is 12' x 4'
12 x 4 = 48 square feet per sheet
1,530 sf ÷ 48 sf = 31.88 sheets
So, 32 sheets are needed
Note that we must have the full extra sheet, even if only a fraction of the sheet will be used

8.   D

$8.39 x 32 = $268.48 subtotal for drywall.
6% sales tax is $268.48 x .06 = $16.11
$268.48 + $16.11 = $284.59

Answer	Solution

B

Bedroom 1 is 12' x 15' with a height of 12'
Two walls are 12' x 12' = 144 square feet each
Two walls are 15' x 12' = 180 square feet each
Ceiling is 12' x 15' = 180 square feet
144 + 144 + 180 + 180 + 180 = 828 total square feet for Bedroom 1

Bedroom 2 is identical to Bedroom 1, so BR 2 is also 828 square feet

Master Bedroom is 35' x 24' with a height of 12'
(We get 35' length because length of home is:
80' – 15' – 30' ((of known other rooms)) = 35')
(We get 24 width' because combined width of BRs 1 & 2 = 24')
Two walls are 35' x 12' = 420 square feet each
Two walls are 24' x 12' = 288 square feet each
Ceiling is 35' x 24' = 840 square feet
420 + 420 + 288 + 288 + 840 = 2,256 total wall/ceiling square feet for Master Bedroom.

Three-bedroom total wall/ceiling square feet is 828 + 828 + 2,256 = 3,912 square feet

10.   A

145 sheets of drywall to be hung:
145 x $2.95 = $427.75
145 sheets needed, but already have 65:
145 – 65 = 80
80 x $8.39 = $671.20
Sales Tax 6%
$671.20 x .06 = $40.27
$671.20 + $40.27 = $711.47 total paid for 80 sheets
The total amount to be invoiced for this is $427.75 + $711.47 = $1,139.22

Excavation and Hauling
Questions and Answers

1. Your job calls for you to excavate a perimeter trench around a pool area that is 3' wide x 4' deep and runs 160 lineal feet. The soil is comprised of heavy soil and clay. You have no option but to excavate this trench by hand and you only have 1 day to get this accomplished. Approximately _____ cubic yards of soil must be excavated. (Select closest answer)

   A. 25
   B. 27
   C. 64
   D. 71

2. For the above question, you will have to hire _____ laborers if an average laborer can excavate an average of 5 cubic yards of heavy soil/clay per day. (Select closest answer)

   A. 15
   B. 17
   C. 22
   D. 24

3. In question 1, _____ laborers would be needed if the soil to be excavated was sandy loam, if a laborer can excavate an average of 6 cubic yards of sandy loam per day. (Select closest answer)

   A. 9
   B. 12
   C. 16
   D. 24

4. In the example in question 1, _____ laborers would be needed if the trench to be excavated was 120 linear feet of heavy soil/clay. (Select closest answer)

   A. 11
   B. 12
   C. 16
   D. 20

5. In question 1, if the 160-foot trench forms a 50' x 30' rectangle, the area inside the rectangle is _____ square feet. (Select closest answer)

   A. 900
   B. 1,200
   C. 1,500
   D. 2,400

6. Your job calls for you to excavate a pit for a pool. The pit must be 30' wide x 50 long and be 12' deep. The soil is comprised of wet clay. You will be using a hydraulic backhoe tractor with a 1.0 cubic yard bucket. _____ cubic yards of material must be removed. Round up any partial cubic yards. (Select closest answer)

    A. 525
    B. 624
    C. 666
    D. 667

7. In the example in question 6, taking into account the swell factor, _____ eight cubic yard capacity truckloads will be required to remove all the material excavated. (Select closest answer)

    A. 21
    B. 78
    C. 84
    D. 100

8. In the example in question 6, the project has to be delayed after excavation. Municipal code requires warning tape be placed around the perimeter of the pit, and that the pit be covered. _____ feet of tape will be needed to surround the pit. (Select closest answer)

    A. 80
    B. 100
    C. 160
    D. 1,500

9. If in the above question, tape comes in 50' rolls costing $11.00 per roll plus 3% tax, _____ must be spent on tape. (Select closest answer)

    A. $11.33
    B. $33.00
    C. $45.32
    D. $67.98

10. In question 6, _____ square feet of material would be required to exactly cover the pit (no overlap). (Select closest answer)

    A. 1,500
    B. 1,560
    C. 1,600
    D. 2,000

Questions 11 – 16 refer to the following job:

A construction job will require a trench for PVC pipe 3' wide, 3'deep, and 250 yards long. Because of accessibility issues, the trench must be hand excavated. The soil is sandy loam. The job must be completed in two regular work days (8 hours per person per day). The labor cost, per man, per whole day, is $110. The trench, by municipal code, must have yellow fluorescent tape around the entire perimeter of the trench after normal working hours. (Select closest answers)

11. _____ cubic yards of material must be excavated.

    A. 198
    B. 225
    C. 250
    D. 750

12. _____ laborers will be needed to complete the job within the required time if a laborer can excavate an average of 6 cu yds of sandy loam per day.

    A. 20
    B. 21
    C. 28
    D. 32

13. The cost of manpower would be _____. (Laborers only, no partial day payments)

    A. $3,220
    B. $3,690
    C. $4,620
    D. $4,880

14. _____ feet of tape will be required for perimeter of the trench.

    A. 276
    B. 1,506
    C. 2,280
    D. 2,800

15. In the above job, if the labor cost was increased to $120.00 per day per man, instead of $110, _____ extra would have to be spent.

    A. $320
    B. $420
    C. $462
    D. $488

16. An excavation job was completed, leaving 24 cubic yards of wet gravel that has a swell factor of 15%. You've been hired to remove the gravel in your truck, which can carry 6 cubic yards per load. Allowing for swell, you will need _____ loads to haul all the gravel.

    A. 2
    B. 4
    C. 5
    D. 7

17. In the above example, if the load were Topsoil, allowing for swell factor of 30%, _____ trips will be needed.

    A. 3
    B. 4
    C. 5
    D. 6

18. Your job calls for you to excavate a pit for a foundation. The pit must be 40' wide x 64' long and be 10' deep. The soil is comprised of wet earth (moist loam). You will be using a Hydraulic Backhoe Tractor with a 1.0 Cubic Yard Bucket. Your trucks can haul 10 cubic yards in one load. _____ cubic yards of material must be removed. Round up any partial cubic yards.

    A. 895
    B. 927
    C. 949
    D. 971

19. The excavation should take _____ days. Backhoe can excavate an average of 720 cu. yds of moist loam per day

    A. 1
    B. 2
    C. 3
    D. 5

20. For the above question, allowing for a swell factor of 10%, you will need _____ loads to haul all the gravel.

    A. 86
    B. 97
    C. 101
    D. 105

****Please see Answer Key on the following page****

3/31/22

Excavation and Hauling
Questions and Answers
Answers Key

	Answer	Solution

1.   D

$3 \times 4 \times 160 = 1,920$ cu ft.
1,920 cu ft. $\div 27 = 71.11$ cu yds
(Note: Cubic feet $\div 27 =$ cubic yards)

2.   A

$3 \times 4 \times 160 = 1,920$ cu. ft.
1,920 cu. ft. $\div 27 = 71.11$ cu. yds.
$71.11 \div 5 = 14.22$
So, 15 workers needed.

3.   B

$3 \times 4 \times 160 = 1,920$ cu. ft.
1,920 cu. ft. $\div 27 = 71.11$ cu. yds.
$71.11 \div 6 = 11.85$
So, 12 workers needed

4.   A

$3 \times 4 \times 120 = 1,440$ cu. ft.
1,440 cu. ft. $\div 27 = 53.33$ cu. yds.
$53.33 \div 5 = 10.67$
So, 11 workers needed

5.   C

$30 \times 50 = 1,500$
(Side x Adjoining side = Area of a rectangle)

6.   D

$30 \times 50 \times 12 = 18,000$ cu ft.
$18,000 \div 27$ (27 cu ft per cu yd) $= 666.67$
(Remember the instruction to round up)

7.   D

Total cu. yds. to be hauled is $30 \times 50 \times 12 = 18,000$ cu. ft.
$18,000 \div 27$ (27 cu. ft. per cu. yd.) $= 666.67$
Add swell factor of 20% or 133.333 ($666.67 \times .2$)
$133.33 + 666.67 = 800$
$800 \div 8$ (capacity of truck) $= 100$

8.   C

Perimeter of a rectangle = sum of all four sides
$30 + 50 + 30 + 50 = 160$

9.   C

Perimeter of a rectangle = sum of all four sides
$30 + 50 + 30 + 50 = 160$
So, 4 rolls are needed even though 40 feet will be left over
(3 rolls would only contain 150 feet)
Each roll is $11.00, $11 \times 4 = \$44.00$
Add tax of 3% or $1.32
Total due is $45.32

	Answer	Solution

0.   A   One side x Adjoining side = Area of a rectangle
30 x 50 = 1,500

1.   C   3 x 3 x 750 (250 yd x 3 to get feet) = 6,750 cu. ft.
6,750 cu. ft. ÷ 27 = 250 cu. yds.
(Note: Cubic feet ÷ 27 = Cubic yards)

2.   B   3 x 3 x 750 = 6,750 cu. ft.
6,750 cu. ft. ÷ 27 = 250 cu. yds.
250 ÷ 6 = 41.67
So, 42 workers needed to do the job in one day
But, given two days, it will take 20.83, or 21 workers.

3.   C   3 x 3 x 750 = 6,750 cu. ft.
6,750 cu. ft. ÷ 27 = 250 cu. yds.
250 ÷ 6 = 41.67
So, 42 laborers needed to do the job in one day
But, given two days, it will take 20.83, or 21 laborers
21 x $110.00/day = $2,310.00 x 2 days = $4,620.00

4.   B   Perimeter of a rectangle = sum of all four sides
First convert the length of the trench from yards to feet: (multiply yards by 3)
250 yards x 3 = 750 feet
Add the sum of all four sides: 750 ft. + 750 ft. + 3 ft. + 3 ft. = 1,506 ft

5.   B   Given: a laborer can excavate an average of 6 cu yds. of sandy loam per day
3 x 3 x 750 = 6,750 cu. ft.
6,750 cu. ft. ÷ 27 = 250 cu. yds.
250 ÷ 6 = 41.67
So, 42 laborers needed to do the job in one day.
But, given two days, it will take 20.83, or 21 laborers.
21 x $110.00/day = $2,310.00
$2,310.00 x 2 days = $4,620.00
Substitute $120.00 per day and it's 21 x $120.00 = $2,520
$2,520 x 2 days = $5,040
The difference between 5,040 and 4,620 = 420

16.   C   Total cu. yds. to be hauled is 24.
Add swell factor of 15% or 3.6 cu. yds. (24 x .15)
24 + 3.6 = 27.6.
27.6 ÷ 6 (capacity of truck) = 4.6.
So, 5 trips will be needed, with the last trip being a partial load

17.   D   Total cu. yds. to be hauled is 24
Add swell factor of 30% or 7.2 cu. yds. (24 x .30).
24 + 7.2 = 31.2
31.2 ÷ 6 (capacity of truck) = 5.2.
So, 6 trips will be needed, with the last trip being a partial load.

18.   C   40 x 64 x 10 = 25,600 cu ft.

25,600 cu ft. ÷ 27 = 948.15 cu yds.
(Note: cubic feet ÷ 27 = cubic yards)

Answer	Solution

19.   B   Per table in Walker's, the described Backhoe can excavate an average of 720 cu. yds of moist loam per day. So, if we determined that there are 948.15 cu. yds. to be excavated, i will take 2 days (1,440 cu. yds. possible, but one day is too little – 720 cu. yds.)

20.   D   Total cu. yds. to be hauled is 949
Add swell factor of 10% or 94.9 cu. yds. (949 x .10)
949 + 94.9 = 1,043.9
1,043.9 ÷ 10 (capacity of truck) = 104.39
So, 105 trips will be needed, with the last trip being a partial load.

Concrete Calculations
Practice Exam – 1

1. You are a contractor that is estimating a job for a homeowner that has a driveway measuring 18 feet wide by 50 yards long. The driveway will be 6 inches thick. _____ cubic yards of concrete will need to be ordered.

    A. 20
    B. 45
    C. 50
    D. 60

2. In the above example, if concrete costs $75.00 per cubic yard, the total cost of concrete will be _____.

    A. $3,750
    B. $3,780
    C. $4,000
    D. $4,275

3. You are a contractor that is estimating a job for a homeowner that has a driveway that measures 6 yards wide by 100 yards long. The driveway will be 4 inches thick. _____ cubic yards of concrete will need to be ordered.

    A. 66
    B. 76
    C. 112
    D. A, B, and C are wrong

4. In the above example, if concrete costs $50.00 per cubic yard, the cost of concrete will be _____.

    A. $1,650
    B. $3,300
    C. $3,450
    D. $5,250

5. You are a contractor that is estimating a job for a homeowner that has a driveway that measures 12 feet wide by 300 yards long. The driveway will be 6 inches thick. _____ cubic yards of concrete will need to be ordered.

    A. 90
    B. 160
    C. 200
    D. 220

6. In the above example, if concrete costs $75.00 per cubic yard, the cost of concrete will be _____.

    A. $12,000
    B. $13,000
    C. $14,000
    D. $15,000

7. You are a contractor that is estimating a job for a homeowner that has a driveway that measures 12 feet wide and 120 feet long. The driveway will be 6 inches thick. _____ cubic yards of concrete will need to be ordered.

    A. 22
    B. 24
    C. 26
    D. 27

8. In the above example, if concrete costs $60.00 per cubic yard, the cost of concrete will be _____.

    A. $1,600
    B. $1,620
    C. $1,640
    D. $4,000

9. You are a contractor that is estimating a job for a homeowner that has a driveway that measures 12 yards wide by 12 yards long. The driveway will be 8 inches thick. _____ cubic yards of concrete will need to be ordered.

    A. 20
    B. 25
    C. 28
    D. 33

10. In the above example, if concrete costs $80.00 per cubic yard, the cost of the concrete will be
    _____.

    A. $1,960
    B. $2,640
    C. $2,700
    D. $3,220

11. You are a contractor that is estimating a job for a homeowner that has a driveway that measures 16 yards wide by 60 yards long. The driveway will be 5 inches thick. _____ cubic yards of concrete will need to be ordered.

    A. 106
    B. 128
    C. 135
    D. A, B, and C are wrong

12. In the above example, if concrete costs $75.00 per cubic yard, the cost of concrete will be _____.

    A. $1,065
    B. $1,240
    C. $2,720
    D. $10,125

13. You are a contractor that is estimating a job for a homeowner that has a driveway that measures 6 yards feet wide by 900 feet long. The driveway will be 6 inches thick. _____ cubic yards of concrete will need to be ordered?

    A. 280
    B. 300
    C. 420
    D. 620

14. In the above example, if concrete costs $55.00 per cubic yard, the cost of concrete be will be _____.

    A. $16,500
    B. $17,000
    C. $17,200
    D. $10,125

15. You are a contractor that is estimating a job for a homeowner that has a walkway that measures 30 feet wide by 50 yards long. The driveway will be 1 foot thick. _____ cubic yards of concrete will need to be ordered.

    A. 98
    B. 106
    C. 167
    D. 168

16. In the above example, if concrete costs $50.00 per cubic yard, the cost of concrete will be _____.

    A. $6,300
    B. $8,200
    C. $8,350
    D. $9,900

17. You are a contractor that is estimating a job for a homeowner that has a driveway that measures 18 feet wide by 250 yards long. The concrete will be 6 inches thick. If the surface coating costs the contractor $.95, the cost of resurfacing material will be _____.

    A. $9,288
    B. $10,660
    C. $12,825
    D. $13,825

57

18. You are a contractor that is estimating a job for a homeowner that has a driveway that measures 20 feet wide by 75 yards long. The driveway will be 4 inches thick. _____ cubic yards of concrete will need to be ordered.

    A. 55
    B. 85
    C. 134
    D. 135

19. In the above example, if concrete costs $75.00 per cubic yard, the cost of concrete will be _____.

    A. $3,070
    B. $4,125
    C. $4,525
    D. $5,095

20. You are a contractor that is estimating a job for a homeowner that has a driveway that measures 7 yards wide by 20 yards long. The driveway will be 6 inches thick. _____ cubic yards of concrete will need to be ordered.

    A. 17
    B. 22
    C. 24
    D. 32

****Please see Answer Key on the following page****

ABC 09/21/2021

Concrete Calculations
Practice Exam – 1
Answer Key

	Answer	Solution

1.   C   18 feet x 150 feet (50 yards x 3 feet per yard) x .5 feet (6 inches = 1/2 foot and 1 divided by 2 = .5) = 1,350 cubic feet
1,350 cubic feet divided by 27 (27 cubic feet = 1 cubic yard) = 50 cyd

2.   A   50 cubic yards x $75.00 per cubic yard = $3,750

3.   A   18 feet (6 yards x 3 feet per yard) x 300 feet (100 yards x 3 feet per yard) x .33 feet (4 inches = 1/3 or 4/12 of a foot and 4 divided by 12 = .33) = 1,782 cubic feet.
1,782 cubic feet divided by 27 (27 cubic feet = 1 cubic yard) = 66 cyd

4.   B   66 cubic yards x $50.00 per cubic yard = $3,300

5.   C   12 feet x 900 feet (300 yards x 3 feet per yard) x .5 feet (6 inches = 1/2 foot and 1 divided by 2 = .5) = 5,400 cubic feet
5,400 cubic feet divided by 27 (27 cubic feet = 1 cubic yard) = 200 cyd

6.   D   200 cubic yards x $75.00 per cubic yard = $15,000

7.   D   12 feet x 120 feet x .5 feet (6 inches = 1/2 foot and 1 divided by 2 = .5) = 720 cubic feet.
720 cubic feet divided by 27 (27 cubic feet = 1 cubic yard) = 26.67.
Round up to 27 cyd

8.   B   27 cubic yards x $60.00 per cubic yard = $1,620

9.   D   36 feet (12 yards x 3 feet per yard) x 36 feet (12 yards x 3 feet per yard) x .67 feet (8 inches = 8/12 0r 2/3 foot - 8 divided by 12 = .67) = 868.32 cubic feet
868.32 cubic feet divided by 27 (27 cubic feet = 1 cubic yard) = 32.16 cyd – round up to 33 cyd

10.   B   33 cubic yards x $80.00 per cubic yard = $2,640

11.   C   48 feet (16 yards x 3 feet per yard) x 180 feet (60 yards x 3 feet per yard) x .42 feet (5/12 inches = 5 divided by 12 = .42) = 3,628.88 or 3,629 cubic feet
3,629 cubic feet divided by 27 (27 cubic feet = 1 cubic yard) = 134.4 cyd – round up 135 cyd

12.   D   135 cubic yards x $75.00 per cubic yard = $10,125

	Answer	**Solution**

13.   B   18 feet (6 yards x 3 feet per yard) x 900 feet x .5 feet (6/12 inches = 6 divided by 12 = .5) = 8,100 cubic feet
8,100 cubic feet divided by 27 (27 cubic feet = 1 cubic yard) = 300 cyd

14.   A   300 cubic yards x $55.00 per cubic yard = $1,650

15.   C   30 feet x 150 feet (50 yards x 3 feet per yard) x 1 foot = 4,500 cubic feet
4,500 cubic feet divided by 27 (27 cubic feet = 1 cubic yard) = 166.67 cyd
Round up to 167 cyd

16.   C   167 cubic yards x $50.00 per cubic yard = $8,350

17.   C   18 feet x 750 feet (250 yards x 3 feet per yard) = 13,500 square feet x $.95 = $12,835

18.   A   20 feet x 225 feet (75 yards x 3 feet per yard) x .33 feet (4 inches = 1/3 or 4/12 of a foot and 1 divided by 3 = .33) = 1,485 cubic feet
1,485 cubic feet divided by 27 (27 cubic feet = 1 cubic yard) = 55 cyd

19.   B   55 cubic yards x $75.00 per cubic yard = $4,125

20.   C   21 feet (7 yards x 3 feet per yard) x 60 feet(20 yards x 3 feet per yard) x .5 (6 inches is 1/2 or 6/12 foot and 6 divided by 12 = .5) = 630 cubic feet
630 cubic feet divided by 27 (27 cubic feet = 1 cubic yard) = 23.33 cyd
Round up 24 cyd

Concrete Calculations
Practice Exam – 2

1. You are a contractor that is estimating a job for a homeowner that has a driveway that measures 18 feet wide and 50 yards long. The driveway will be 6 inches thick. What will the cost of resurfacing material be, if the surface coating costs the contractor $.95 per square foot?

    A. $1,990
    B. $2,010
    C. $2,565
    D. $2,600

2. In the above example, what will the cost of surface material be, if surface material costs $.75 per square foot?

    A. $1,080
    B. $2,025
    C. $4,000
    D. $4,275

3. You are a contractor that is estimating a job for a homeowner that has a driveway that measures 6 yards wide and 100 yards long. The driveway will be 4 inches thick. What will the cost of resurfacing material be, if the surface coating costs the contractor $.80 per square foot?

    A. $4,320
    B. $4,360
    C. $4,400
    D. None of the above

4. In the above example, what will the cost of surface material be, if surface material costs $.76 per square foot?

    A. $4,000
    B. $4,104
    C. $4,450
    D. $5,250

5. You are a contractor that is estimating a job for a homeowner that has a driveway that measures 12 feet wide and 300 yards long. The driveway will be 6 inches thick. What will the cost of resurfacing material be, if the surface coating costs the contractor $1.15 per square foot?

   A. $10,080
   B. $12,025
   C. $12,420
   D. $13,275

6. In the above example, what will the cost of surface material be, if surface material costs $1.20 per square foot?

   A. $12,000
   B. $12,420
   C. $12,560
   D. $12,960

7. You are a contractor that is estimating a job for a homeowner that has a driveway that measures 12 feet wide and 120 feet long. The driveway will be 6 inches thick. What will the cost of resurfacing material be, if the surface coating costs the contractor $.78 per square foot?

   A. $980.82
   B. $1,000.00
   C. $1,005.99
   D. $1,123.20

8. In the above example, what will the cost of surface material be, if surface material costs $.85 per square foot?

   A. $1,110
   B. $1,224
   C. $1,640
   D. $2,125

9. You are a contractor that is estimating a job for a homeowner that has a driveway that measures 12 yards wide and 12 yards long. The driveway will be 8 inches thick. What will the cost of resurfacing material be, if the surface coating costs the contractor $.95 per square foot? (round to the nearest dollar)

   A. $1,110
   B. $1,125
   C. $1,231
   D. $1,232

10. In the above example, what will the cost of surface material be, if surface material costs $.1.02 per square foot (round to the nearest dollar)?

   A. $1,230
   B. $1,322
   C. $1,422
   D. $1,888

11. You are a contractor that is estimating a job for a homeowner that has a driveway that measures 48 feet wide and 60 yards long. The driveway will be 5 inches thick. What will the cost of resurfacing material be, if the surface coating costs the contractor $.65 per square foot?

    A. $5,082
    B. $5,525
    C. $5,608
    D. $5,616

12. In the above example, what will the cost of surface material be, if surface material costs $.75 per square foot?

    A. $5,765
    B. $5,998
    C. $6,028
    D. $6,480

13. You are a contractor that is estimating a job for a homeowner that has a driveway that measures 6 yards feet wide and 900 feet long. The driveway will be 6 inches thick. What will the cost of resurfacing material be, if the surface coating costs the contractor $1.25 per square foot?

    A. $20,185
    B. $20,250
    C. $20,750
    D. $22,120

14. In the above example, what will the cost of surface material be, if surface material costs $1.20 per square foot?

    A. $19,440
    B. $19,600
    C. $19,720
    D. $20,025

15. You are a contractor that is estimating a job for a homeowner that has a walkway that measures 30 feet wide and 50 yards long. The driveway will be 1 foot thick. What will the cost of resurfacing material be, if the surface coating costs the contractor $.85 per square foot?

    A. $3,600
    B. $3,820
    C. $3,825
    D. $3,975

16. In the above example, what will the cost of surface material be, if surface material costs $.80 per square foot?

    A. $3,400
    B. $3,500
    C. $3,600
    D. $3,700

17. You are a contractor that is estimating a job for a homeowner that has a driveway that measures 18 feet wide and 250 yards long. The concrete will be 6 inches thick. What will the cost of resurfacing material be, if the surface coating costs the contractor $.55 per square foot?

    A. $6,288
    B. $7,366
    C. $7,425
    D. $7,825

18. In the above example, what will the cost of surface material be, if surface material costs $.77 per square foot?

    A. $12,150
    B. $12,200
    C. $12,330
    D. $12,900

19. You are a contractor that is estimating a job for a homeowner that has a driveway that measures 7 yards wide and 20 yards long. The driveway will be 6 inches thick. What will the cost of resurfacing material be, if the surface coating costs the contractor $1.00 per square foot?

    A. $1,070
    B. $1,260
    C. $1,280
    D. $1,300

20. In the above example, what will the cost of surface material be, if surface material costs $.70 per square foot?

    A. $780
    B. $800
    C. $882
    D. $890

****Please see Answer Key on the following page****

Concrete Calculations - 2
Questions and Answers
Answer Key

	Answer	Solution
1.	C	18 feet x 150 feet (50 yards x 3 feet per yard) = 2,700. 2,700 x \$.95 = \$2,565
2.	B	2,700 x \$.75 per square foot = \$2,025
3.	A	18 feet (6 yards x 3 feet per yard) x 300 feet (100 yards x 3 feet per yard) = 5,400 5,400 x \$.80 per square foot = \$4,320
4.	B	5,400 x \$.76 per square foot = \$4,104
5.	C	12 feet x 900 feet (300 yards x 3 feet per yard) x = 10,800 10,800 x \$1.15 per square foot = \$12,420
6.	D	10,800 square feet x \$1.20 per square foot = \$12,960
7.	D	12 feet x 120 feet x \$.78 = \$1,123.20
8.	B	1,440 x \$.85 per square foot = \$1,224
9.	C	36 feet (12 yards x 3 feet per yard) x 36 feet (12 yards x 3 feet per yard) x \$.95 =\$1,231.20
10.	B	1,296 x \$1.02 per square foot = \$1,321.92
11.	D	48 feet x 180 feet (60 yards x 3 feet per yard) x \$.65 = \$5,616
12.	D	8,640 x \$.75 per square foot = \$6,480
13.	B	18 feet (6 yards x 3 feet per yard) x 900 feet x \$1.25 = \$ 20,250
14.	A	16,200 x \$1.20 per square foot = \$19,440
15.	C	30 feet x 150 feet (50 yards x 3 feet per yard) x \$.85 = \$3,825
16.	C	4,500 x \$.80 per square foot = \$3,600
17.	C	18 feet x 750 feet (250 yards x 3 feet per yard) = 13,500 square feet x \$.55 = \$7,425
18.	A	13,500 square feet x \$.90 per square foot = \$12,150
19.	B	21 feet (7 yards x 3 feet per yard) x 60 feet (20 yards x 3 feet per yard) = 1,260 sq. feet 1,260 sq. feet x \$1.00 = \$1,260
20.	C	1,260 x \$.70 per square foot = \$882

General, Building and Residential Contractor
Math Practice Test

1. The total tons of 18J5 joists required for the roof-framing plan is _____. 18J5 joists weigh 9.8 pounds per linear foot. *** Refer to roof-framing plan at end of exam ***

   A. Less than 6.5
   B. Between 6.5 and 7.0
   C. Between 7.0 and 7.5
   D. More than 7.5

2. The parking lot needs to be enlarged. The architect wishes to extend the parking lot to within 5 feet of the east property line. Twenty additional parking spaces will be provided. A formal Change Order was agreed to by all parties. The following prices are available as of the date of the Change Order: ***Refer to Site Plan (partial) at end of exam***

   -Asphalt $7.30 per square yard including base
   -Curbing $4.80 per lineal foot
   -Parking stops $35 each including rods

   The materials total cost for the change order is _____.

   A. Less than $7,400
   B. Between $7,400 and $7,600
   C. Between $7,600 and $7,800
   D. More than $7,800

3. Sod cost $1.80 per 216 square inches. The total cost to sod Sodded Area Number 3 is _____.

   A. Less than $6,000
   B. Between $6,000 and $6,500
   C. Between $6,500 and $7,000
   D. More than $7,000

4. All restroom ceiling heights are 9 feet. CMU extends 8 inches above the finished ceiling. The total of 4-inch CMU required for the restrooms depicted on partial floor plan page 4 of 6 is _____.

   A. Less than 320
   B. Between 320 and 340
   C. Between 340 and 360
   D. More than 360

5. The lineal feet of fencing required for the 100-foot radius portion of the storage yard is _____.
   Fencing is 8 feet high with razor wire topping. Do not include the gate fencing. ***Refer to Storage Yard Plan (partial) at end of exam***

   A. Less than 100
   B. Between 100 and 150
   C. Between 150 and 200
   D. More than 200

6. The total cubic yards of concrete required to place the entrance steps is _____.

   A. Less than 6.5
   B. Between 6.5 and 7.0
   C. Between 7.0 and 7.5
   D. More than 7.5

7. The total cubic yards of concrete required to construct the curbing for the parking lot is _____.

   A. Less than 24
   B. Between 24 and 26
   C. Between 26 and 28
   D. More than 28

8. The total tons of rebar required for the grade beams is _____. Allow for waste factor of 2%.

   A. Less than 1.7
   B. Between 1.7 and 1.8
   C. Between 1.8 and 1.9
   D. More than 1.9

9. The total number of working days for the critical path is _____.

   A. 187
   B. 197
   C. 192
   D. 195

10. A steel beam has a 13.28 in^2 cross section. The encased column measures 14" x 14" x 14' high. The total volume of concrete required to encase the column is _____ cubic feet.

    A. Less than 18
    B. Between 18 and 19
    C. Between 19 and 20
    D. More than 20

11. A standard modular face brick wall is 100 feet by 300 feet. The mortar joint is 3/8" thick. The wall requires 6.75 bricks per square feet of wall area. The total cubic feet of mortar required to erect the wall is _____.

    A. 300
    B. 500
    C. 1,064
    D. 1,641

12. The total capacity of all six piles supporting one Number 2 pile cap is _____ tons. The soil bearing capacity is 7,750 pounds per square foot. The shear resistance for the soil is 630 pounds per square foot. Each pile is 21 feet long, 14 inches in average diameter with a 12-inch tip for driving.

    A. Less than 145
    B. Between 145 and 155
    C. Between 155 and 165
    D. More than 165

13. Rob a brick mason and Charlie his helper place an average of 1,500 standard bricks per eight-hour day. Rob charges $22.50 per hour and Charlie charges $10.50 per hour. A double wythe wall 6 feet high, 30 feet long is to be built. Bricks cost $750 per thousand. The owner wants a 3/8ths inch bed joint. The total labor cost for the wall is _____.

    A. Less than $430
    B. Between $430 and $450
    C. Between $450 and $470
    D. More than $470

14. Given:

    - A 19-foot long woodpile
    - Earth shear factor 325 psf
    - Bearing capacity 3000 psf
    - 14-inch diameter with a 10-inch tip
    - 4 piles supporting an elevator pit

The total shear capacity is _____ pounds.

    A. Less than 88,000
    B. Between 88,000 and 92,000
    C. Between 92,000 and 96,000
    D. More than 96,000

15. A gable duplex must have fire separation protection as required by code. The rise and run is 5 in 12. The span including the overhang is 64 feet typical. Living areas are ninety degrees to the ridgeline. The overhang is 2 feet continuous on all sides. The total square feet above the ceiling to be fireproofed on one side only is _____.

    A. Less than 350
    B. Between 350 and 400
    C. Between 400 and 450
    D. More than 450

16. Two- and three-quarter acres must be cleared of light brush and tree saplings before construction may begin. ABC Construction plans to hire XYZ Bulldozer Inc. to do the clearing. XYZ advises ABC they will use a 90-horsepower diesel bulldozer. XYZ also advises ABC that ABC must supply the diesel. The maximum gallons of diesel ABC should expect to purchase for the clearing work is _____.

    A. Less than 300
    B. Between 300 and 320
    C. Between 320 and 340
    D. More than 340

17. A retention pond must be dug in Class "B" soil determined by thumb penetration test. The retention pond will be 10 feet deep and measure 64 feet by 32 feet. The total cubic yards of dirt to be removed is _____. Do not consider the 25 percent swell factor for the excavation.

    A. Less than 200
    B. Between 200 and 220
    C. Between 220 and 240
    D. More than 240

18. Given a benchmark reading of 32.56, a first reading of 5.6, a back sight reading of 5.1, a backswing reading of 4.3, a foresight reading of 9.2, a foresight reading of 2.2 and a front swing reading of 3.7, the ground elevation should be _____.

    A. 26.66
    B. 32.46
    C. 28.96
    D. 32.66

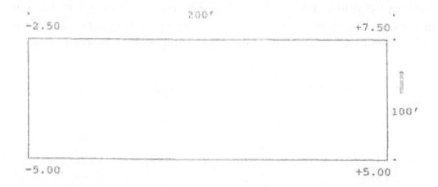

19. The property above is to be graded to a uniform flat elevation of -1.50'. No fill is brought to the lot from the outside of the property lines. The total net volume of cut removed from the property lines is _____ cubic yards. Make no allowance for expansion of cut material (swell) during excavation.

    A. Less than 1,750
    B. Between 1,750 and 1,950
    C. Between 1,951 and 2,150
    D. More than 2,150

20. The 10' by 10' by 14-inch thick foundation of an elevator pit is to be supported by four (4) piles. The piles are required to support a load of 90.4 tons through the use of skin friction and end bearing. The following conditions apply:

- Skin friction   750 psf
- Soil bearing   6000 psf
- Pile size, tip diameter   8 inches
- Pile size, average diameter   12 inches

The average pile length required is how many feet _____. Pile length is to be rounded to the nearest foot.

    A. 18
    B. 19
    C. 20
    D. 21

21. Given the following information:

    -Swell factor is 25 percent
    -Crawler tractor equipment
    -Heaped bucket capacity is 3/4 cubic yards
    -Fixed cycle time is 2.6 minutes
    -Round trip distance is 280 feet
    -Speed is 1.5 miles per hour

    Using the information given, the hourly production in cubic yards is _____.

    A. 6
    B. 7
    C. 8
    D. 9

22. A pit is to be excavated using a 2 cubic yard bucket dozer with a 45-minute hour efficiency. The loam soil has a swell factor of 25 percent. The cycle time for both travel and fixed operation is 4.8 minutes including loading, dumping and turning. The production in cubic yards per hour is _____.

    A. 10 to 12
    B. 12 to 14
    C. 14 to 16
    D. 16 to 18

23. A contractor is performing an estimate on a building with drawings scaled to 3/8" = 1' 0". The contractor then measures 4 (7/8)" on the drawings. The actual measurement of the building is _____.

    A. 8' 6"
    B. 12' 0"
    C. 13' 0"
    D. 14' 6"

****Please see Answer Key on the following page****
ABC 09/21/2021

71

General, Building and Residential Contractor
Math Practice Test
Answer Key

Q	A	Solution

1.   **C**   Number of joists x L x WPLF ÷ 2,000 lbs. in a ton = Tons   Roof Framing Plan

         48 x 19.33 ft x 9.8 #/lf   = 9,092.83 lbs.   (14+14+10+10)
         26 x 20 ft x 9.8 #/lf   = 5,096.00 lbs.   (10+10+6)
          2 x 11.33 ft x 9.8 #/lf   = <u>222.06 lbs.</u>   (20ft – 8'8")
                                       14,410.89 lbs. ÷ 2,000 lbs. in a ton = **7.205 tons**

2.   **C**   48.33   -   5   =   43.33   Site Plan (partial)
         45   +   30   +   90   = 165.00
         Area of asphalt – Length x Width
         Asphalt – 43.33 ft x 165 ft   = 7,149.45 ft^2 / 9 ft^2 = 794.38 yd^2
         Asphalt cost – 794.38 yd^2 x $7.30 per yd^2 = $5,798.99
         Perimeter =   1 new side x Length + 2 x Width
         Perimeter = 1 x 165 ft + 2 x 43.33 ft = 251.66 ft
         Curbing cost – 251.66 ft x $4.80 per ft   = $1,207.97
         Parking stops – 20 x $35 each   = <u>$ 700.00</u>
                                                         = **$7,706.96**

3.   **A**   Walker's Building Estimator's Reference Book, 31st Edition, page 1399 and Site Plan (Partial)
         Area of a circle – Subtract the smaller one from the larger one divide by 4
         Area 1 = π r ^{2} = π (120 ft – 1.5 ft) ^{2} and   Area 2 = π r ^{2} = π (90 ft) ^{2}
         Area 1 = 44,115.03 ft^2 -   25,446.90 ft^2 = 18,668.13 / 4 =   4,667.03   ft^2
         4,667.03 ft^2 x $1.80/216 in^2 x 144 in^2 / ft^2 = **$5,600.44**

4.   **B**   Walker's Building Estimator's Reference Book, 31st Edition, pages 512 and 519 & Floor
         Plan (Partial)
         16 ft (center line to center line) minus ½ (8" CMU each side) = 16 ft – 2(4") = 15.33 ft long
         Number of walls x L x H x 112.5/100 sq. ft of wall = CMU
         2 X 15.33 ft x 9.67 high x 1.125 = 333.54 or **334 CMU's**

5.   **C**   Walker's Building Estimator's Reference Book, 31st Edition, page 1397 and Storage
         Yard Plan
         Circumference = 2 π r - 2 x 3.14 x 100ft ÷ 4 = **157.08 ft**

6.   **D**   Walker's Building Estimator's Reference Book, 31st Edition - pages 277 and 519 & Partial
         First Floor Plan Sheet
         Volume of concrete = Lineal feet of stairs x Area
         Lineal ft of stairs   19 - 5 + 20 + 4 = 38 ft
         Take total area of concrete side view and subtract non-concrete area
         Area = 4 ft x 22" / 12" per ft = 7.33 ft^2 subtract   3 x (1 ft x .5 ft) = 1.5 ft^2
         Area of concrete side view = 7.33 ft^2 -   1.5 ft^2 = 5.83 ft^2
         Volume of concrete - (38 ft x 5.83 ft^2) ÷ 27 ft^3 / yd^3 = **8.20 yd^3**

Q	A	Solution

7.   B   Walker's Building Estimator's Reference Book, 31st Edition, page 1397 and Site Plan (partial)
90 + 170 - 48.33 + 45 + 30 + 90 + 170 - 48.33 - 30 = 468.34 ft
Circumference = 2 π r - (2 x 3.14 x (120 ft - 1.5 ft)) / 4 = 186.045 ft
Total lineal footage – 468.34 ft + 186.045 ft = 654.385 ft
Note: A 1 foot 6-inch curb has an area of 1.04 square feet
Total amount of concrete – 654.385 ft x 1.04 ft^2 = 680.056 ft^3 / 27 ft^3 per yd^3 = **25.205 yd^3**

8.   B   Walker's Building Estimator's Reference Book, 31st Edition, pages 258 and Foundation Plan
Perimeter of foundation plan – (2 x 80) + (2 x (19+1)) + (2 x (1 +19 + 20 + 20 + 1)) = 322 ft
\# Beams x \# Bars x L x WPLF ÷ 2,000 lbs. in a ton = tons of rebar
1 x 10 x 322 ft x 1.043lbs per foot = 3,358.46 lbs. x waste factor of 2% = 3,425.63 lbs.
3,425.63 lbs. ÷ 2,000 lbs. in ton = **1.71 tons**

9.   B   Walker's Building Estimator's Reference Book, 31st Edition, page 122 and Construction Activity Network Plan Sheet
10 + 12 + 16 + 18 + 32 + 13 +24 + 34 + 13 + 14 + 11= **197 days**

10.   A   Walker's Building Estimator's Reference Book, 31st Edition, page 1397
\# of columns x L x W x H = CF
1 x 1.17 ft x 1.17 ft x 14ft = 19.16 ft^3
Subtract the steel beam
Note: Cross section is square inches; 13.28 in^2 ÷ 144 in^2 per ft^2 = .092 ft^2
1 x .092 ft^2 x 14 ft = 1.29 ft^3
19.16 ft^3 - $^{1.29}$ ft^3 = **17.87 ft^3**

11.   D   Walker's Building Estimator's Reference Book, 31st Edition, pages 450 and 451
300 ft^x 100 ft x 6.75 units per ft^2 x 8.1 ft^3 per 1,000 units = **1,640.25 ft^3**

12.   C   Principles/Practices of Commercial Construction, 10th, page 117
Principles/Practices of Commercial Construction, 9th, page 114
End area = π x D^2 /4
The tip diameter of the pile in feet = 12"/12" = 1 ft
3.14 x 1 ft^2 / 4 = .785 ft^2
End Bearing Capacity = 7,750 lbs. / ft^2 x .785 ft^2 = 6,083.75 lbs.
The average pipe circumference in feet = π x D
3.14 x 14"/12" = 3.67 ft
Effective pile surface area = pile effective length x average circumference
Effective pile surface area = 21 ft x 3.67 ft = 77.07 ft^2
Shear capacity of soil = shear strength of soil x effective pile surface area
Shear capacity of soil = 630 lbs. per ft^2 x 77.07 ft^2 = 48,554.10 lbs.
Total capacity of one pile = 6,083.75 lbs. + 48,554.10 lbs. = 54,637.85 lbs.
Total capacity of all six piles = 54,637.85 lbs. /2000 lbs. per ton x 6 = **163.9 tons**

Q	**A**	**Solution**

13.   A   Walker's Building Estimator's Reference Book, 31st Edition, page 433
Labor cost - $22.50 + $10.50 = $ 33.00 per hour
Wall to be built – 6 ft x 30 ft x 13.33 bricks per one square ft of wall = 2,399.4 bricks
2,399.4 bricks ÷ 1,500 bricks in a day = 1.59 days
1.59 days x 8 hrs. in a day = 12.72 hours
12.72 hrs. x $33.00 per hour = **$419.76**

14.   B   Principles/Practices of Commercial Construction, 10th, page 117
Principles/Practices of Commercial Construction, 9th, page 114
Total shear capacity = Shear strength x Effective pile surface area
Effective pile surface area = Pile effective length in feet x average pile circumference in feet
Average pile circumference = π x D = 3.14 x 14"/12" = 3.665 ft
19 ft x 3.665 ft = 69.635 ft^2
Total shear capacity = 325 lbs. per ft^2 x 69.635 ft^2 x 4 piles = **90,525.50 lbs.**

15.   B   Walker's Building Estimator's Reference Book, 31st Edition, page 786
64 ft - 2 ft overhang one side – 2 ft overhang other side = 60 ft Span – length of rafter
60 ft / 2 = 30 ft Common Run
30 ft x (5 ÷ 12) = 12.5 ft length of ridge
One side divide by 2 = (60 ft x 12.5 ft) / 2 = **375 ft^2**

16.   D   Walker's Building Estimator's Reference Book, 31st edition, pages 1346 and 1359
2.75 acres x 43,560 ft^2 in an acre = 119,790 ft^2
119,790 ft^2 / 1,250 ft^2 per hour = 95.83 hrs.
90 hp engine estimated to consume per hour – 90 hp x .040 = 3.6 gallons per hour
95.83 hrs. x 3.6 gallons per hour = **344.99 gallons**

17.   A   Walker's Building Estimator's Reference Book, 31st Edition, page 1444 and Principals/Practices
Commercial Construction, 9th, page 72
Class "B" soil / use slope 1: 1
Volume = (A$_1$ + A$_{2)}$) / 2 x L
Top area A$_1$ = 64 ft x 32 ft = 2,048 ft^2
Bottom A$_2$ = (64 ft – 10 ft) x (32 ft – 10 ft) = 1,188 ft^2
Distance between the two areas = 10 ft
Volume = (2,048 ft^2 - 1,188 ft^2) / 2 x 10 ft = 4,300 ft^3 / 27 ft^3 per yd^3 = **159.26 yd^3**

18.   B   Principles/Practices of Commercial Construction, 10th, pages 51 – 52
Principles/Practices of Commercial Construction, 9th, pages 24-47
BM + BS - FS = GE
32.56 + 5.6 + 5.1 + 4.3 - 9.2 - 2.2 - 3.7 = 32.46

19.   C   Walker's Building Estimator's Reference Book, 31st Edition, page 1253
Cross Sectional Method - Average Elevation: (7.5ft + 5ft - 5ft - 2.5ft) / 4 = +1.25ft
+1.25 to -1.50 = 2.75 Cut
L x W x D = Volume / 27 ft^3 per yd^3
(200 ft x 100 ft x 2.75 ft) / 27 ft^3 per yd^3 = **2,037.03 yd^3**

2	A	**Solution**

20. B Principles/Practices of Commercial Construction, 10th, page 117
Principles/Practices of Commercial Construction, 9th, page 114
Load / 4 piles = tons per pile x 2000 lbs. in a ton = lbs. per pile
90.4 tons / 4 piles = 22.6 tons x 2,000 lbs. per ton = 45,200 lbs. per pile
End area = π x D^2 /4 and 8/12 = .67 ft
End area = 3.14 x (.67)^2 / 4 = .35 ft^2
End bearing capacity = Soil bearing capacity x End area
End bearing capacity = 6,000 lbs. per ft^2 x .35 ft^2 = 2,100 lbs.
The average pipe circumference in feet = π x D
3.14 x 12"/12" = 3.14 ft

Work backwards
Total pile capacity = 45,200 lbs. per pile – 2,100 lbs. per pile = 43,100 lbs. per pile
Shear capacity of soil = shear strength of soil x effective pile surface area
43,100 lbs. = 750 lbs. / ft^2 x effective pile length in feet x 3.14
Effective pile length = 42,100 lbs. / 750 lbs. per ft^2 / 3.14
Effective pile length = 17.87 or 18 ft

21. B Principles/Practices of Commercial Construction, 10th, pages 76 – 80
Principles/Practices of Commercial Construction, 9th, pages 91 – 93
Production (yd^3 / hr.) = E (min/hr.) x I (shrinkage factor) x H (yd^3)
　　　　　　　　　　　　　　　　　　　C (min)

Shrinkage factor (I) = $\frac{1}{1 + \% \text{ Swell} /100}$ = 1 / (1 + 25/100) = .8

Cycle time = CT + CF
CT = D / (S x 88) = 280 ft / (1.5 miles x 88) = 2.12 min + 2.6 min = 4.72 min

Production (yd^3) = $\frac{50 \text{ min/hr. x .8 x .75 yd}^3}{4.72 \text{ min}}$ = **6.35 yd^3 / hr.** round up

22. C Principles/Practices of Commercial Construction, 10th, pages 76 – 80
Principles/Practices of Commercial Construction, 9th, pages 91 – 93
Production (yd^3 / hr.) = E (min/hr.) x I (shrinkage factor) x H (yd^3)
　　　　　　　　　　　　　　　　　　　C (min)

Shrinkage factor (I) = $\frac{1}{1 + \% \text{ Swell} /100}$ = 1 / (1 + 25/100) = .8

Cycle time = CT + CF = 4.8 min
Efficiency – 45 min/hr.

Production (yd^3) = $\frac{45 \text{ min/hr. x .8 x 2 yd}^3}{4.8 \text{ min}}$ = **15 yd^3 / hr.**

23. C 4 7/8 divided by 3/8
39/8 x 8/3 = **13 ft**

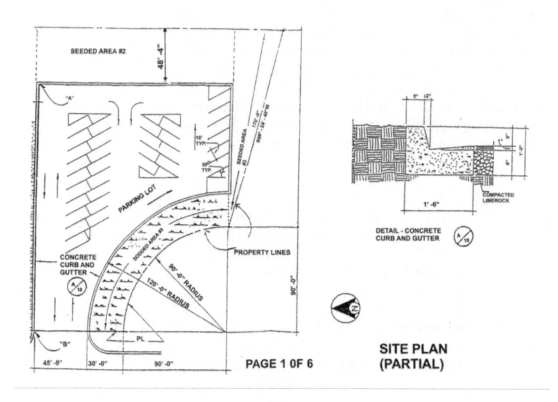

DETAIL - CONCRETE
CURB AND GUTTER (A/18)

SITE PLAN
(PARTIAL)

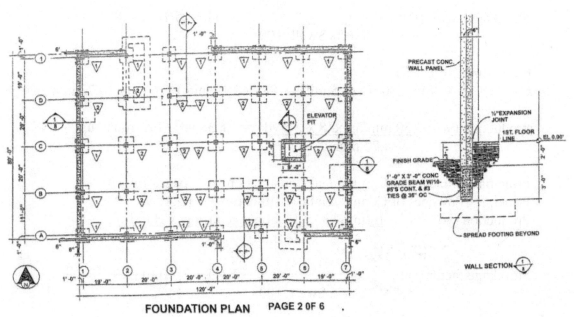

PRECAST CONC.
WALL PANEL

½"EXPANSION
JOINT

1ST. FLOOR
LINE   EL 0.00'

FINISH GRADE

1'-0" X 3'-0" CONC
GRADE BEAM W/10-
#5'S CONT. & #3
TIES @ 36" OC

SPREAD FOOTING BEYOND

WALL SECTION (1/8)

ELEVATOR
PIT

FOUNDATION PLAN   PAGE 2 OF 6

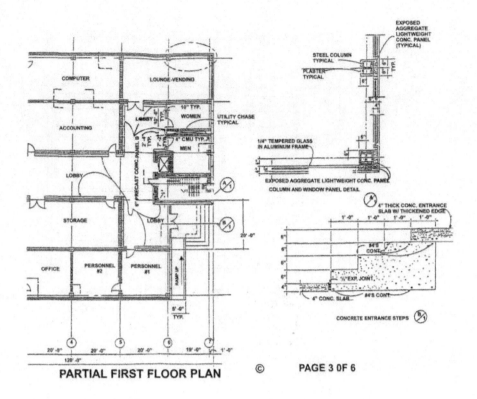

PARTIAL FIRST FLOOR PLAN

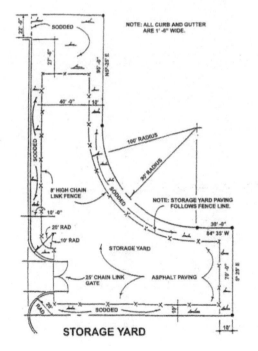

STORAGE YARD

NOTE: ALL CURB AND GUTTER ARE 1'-6" WIDE.

NOTE: STORAGE YARD PAVING FOLLOWS FENCE LINE.

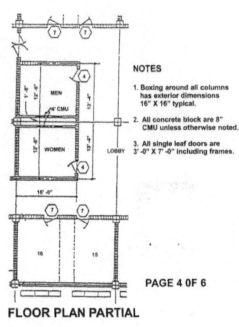

NOTES

1. Boxing around all columns has exterior dimensions 16" X 16" typical.

2. All concrete block are 8" CMU unless otherwise noted.

3. All single leaf doors are 3'-0" X 7'-0" including frames.

PAGE 4 OF 6

FLOOR PLAN PARTIAL

77

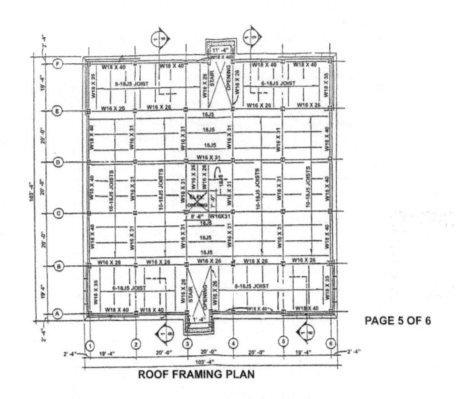

PAGE 5 OF 6

ROOF FRAMING PLAN

ACTIVITY	NETWORK SYMBOL	ACTIVITY	NETWORK SYMBOL	ACTIVITY	NETWORK SYMBOL
AWARD OF CONTRACT PROCEDURES	A	FINAL INSPECTION	N	PILE DRIVING	Z
ASPHALTIC CONCRETE SURFACE	B	FINISH FLOORING AND MOLDING	O	PLANTER CONSTRUCTION	AA
BLOCK MASONRY	C	HARDWARE AND FIXTURES	P	PLUMBING FINISH	BB
CEILING INSTALLATION	D	HEATING, VENTILATING AND AIR CONDITIONING INSTALLATION	Q	PLUMBING - ROUGH IN	CC
CLEAN UP	E			ROOFING	DD
CONCRETE CURB AND WALKS	F	INSULATION	R	SITE CLEARING AND GRUBBING	EE
CONCRETE FLOOR SLABS	G	LANDSCAPING	S	SITE SURVEY - BUILDING LAYOUT	FF
CONCRETE FOUNDATION SYSTEMS ELVA. PITS	H	MATERIALS ORDERED AND DELIVERED	T	SITE SURVEY - EXTERIOR IMPROVEMENTS	GG
CONCRETE PRECAST PANEL INSTALLATION	I	MECHANICAL - ELEVATOR	U	STAIRWAY INSTALLATION	HH
EARTHWORK BACKFILL	J	PAINTING	V	STRUCTURAL STEEL AND STEEL BAR JOISTS	JJ
EARTHWORK EXCAVATION	K	PARTITION AND DRYWALL INSTALLATION	W	TRIM	JJ
ELECTRICAL FINISH	L	PAVING SUBGRADE AND BASE COURSE	X	UTILITIES - SITE	KK
ELECTRICAL ROUGH-IN	M	PERMIT APPLICATION TIME	Y	WINDOWS AND DOORS	LL

LEGEND

CIRCLES WITH NUMBERS INSIDE ARE NODES REPRESENTING THE START AND FINISH OF EACH ACTIVITY.

A LETTER WITH A NUMBER UNDERNEATH REPRESENTS AN ACTIVITY AND ITS DURATION.

DASHED LINES HAVE NO TIME DURATION BUT SHOW THE RELATIONSHIP OF THE ACTIVITY TO OTHER WORK.

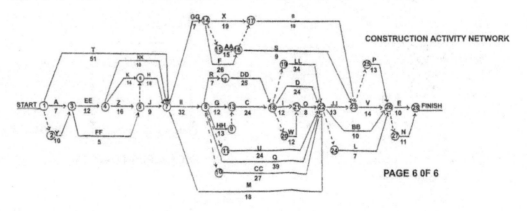

CONSTRUCTION ACTIVITY NETWORK

PAGE 6 OF 6

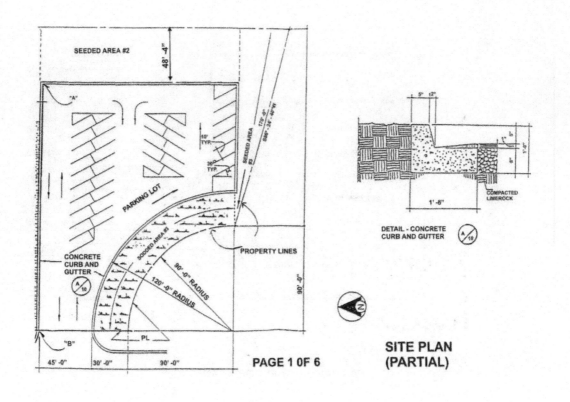

DETAIL - CONCRETE
CURB AND GUTTER

SITE PLAN
(PARTIAL)

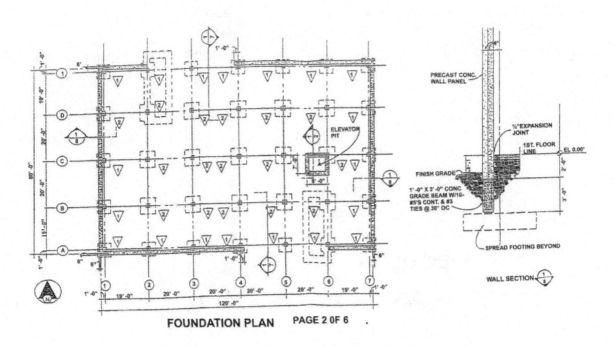

PRECAST CONC.
WALL PANEL

½"EXPANSION
JOINT

1ST. FLOOR
LINE

EL 0.00'

FINISH GRADE

1'-0" X 3'-0" CONC
GRADE BEAM W/10-
#5'S CONT. & #3
TIES @ 36" OC

SPREAD FOOTING BEYOND

WALL SECTION

ELEVATOR
PIT

FOUNDATION PLAN   PAGE 2 OF 6

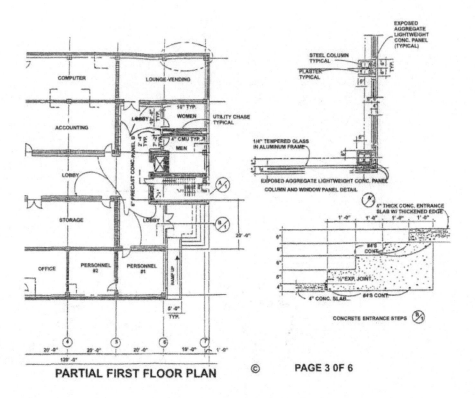

PARTIAL FIRST FLOOR PLAN

EXPOSED AGGREGATE LIGHTWEIGHT CONC. PANEL (TYPICAL)

STEEL COLUMN TYPICAL

PLASTER TYPICAL

1/4" TEMPERED GLASS IN ALUMINUM FRAME

EXPOSED AGGREGATE LIGHTWEIGHT CONC. PANEL

COLUMN AND WINDOW PANEL DETAIL

4" THICK CONC. ENTRANCE SLAB W/ THICKENED EDGE

CONCRETE ENTRANCE STEPS

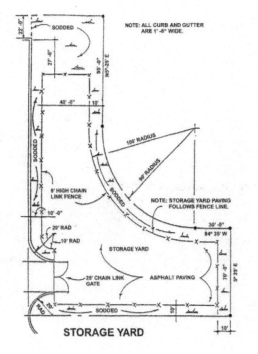

NOTE: ALL CURB AND GUTTER ARE 1'-6" WIDE.

100' RADIUS
90' RADIUS

8' HIGH CHAIN LINK FENCE

NOTE: STORAGE YARD PAVING FOLLOWS FENCE LINE.

20' RAD
10' RAD

STORAGE YARD

25' CHAIN LINK GATE

ASPHALT PAVING

SODDED

STORAGE YARD

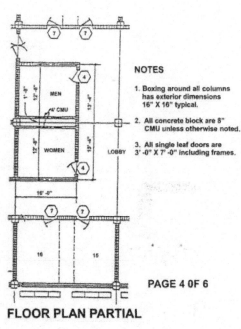

NOTES

1. Boxing around all columns has exterior dimensions 16" X 16" typical.

2. All concrete block are 8" CMU unless otherwise noted.

3. All single leaf doors are 3'-0" X 7'-0" including frames.

MEN

WOMEN

LOBBY

FLOOR PLAN PARTIAL

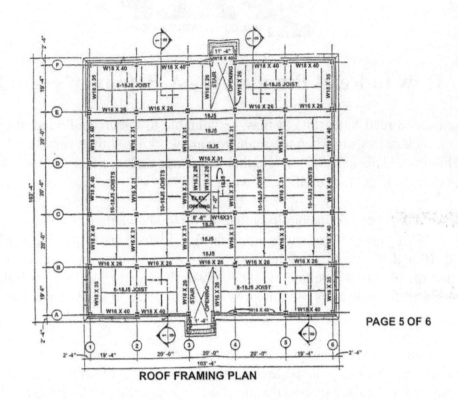

ROOF FRAMING PLAN

ACTIVITY	NETWORK SYMBOL	ACTIVITY	NETWORK SYMBOL	ACTIVITY	NETWORK SYMBOL
AWARD OF CONTRACT PROCEDURES	A	FINAL INSPECTION	N	PILE DRIVING	Z
ASPHALTIC CONCRETE SURFACE	B	FINISH FLOORING AND MOLDING	O	PLANTER CONSTRUCTION	AA
BLOCK MASONRY	C	HARDWARE AND FIXTURES	P	PLUMBING FINISH	BB
CEILING INSTALLATION	D	HEATING, VENTILATING AND AIR CONDITIONING INSTALLATION	Q	PLUMBING - ROUGH IN	CC
CLEAN UP	E			ROOFING	DD
CONCRETE CURB AND WALKS	F	INSULATION	R	SITE CLEARING AND GRUBBING	EE
CONCRETE FLOOR SLABS	G	LANDSCAPING	S	SITE SURVEY - BUILDING LAYOUT	FF
CONCRETE FOUNDATION SYSTEMS ELVA. PITS	H	MATERIALS ORDERED AND DELIVERED	T	SITE SURVEY - EXTERIOR IMPROVEMENTS	GG
CONCRETE PRECAST PANEL INSTALLATION	I	MECHANICAL - ELEVATOR	U	STAIRWAY INSTALLATION	HH
EARTHWORK BACKFILL	J	PAINTING	V	STRUCTURAL STEEL AND STEEL BAR JOISTS	II
EARTHWORK EXCAVATION	K	PARTITION AND DRYWALL INSTALLATION	W	TRIM	JJ
ELECTRICAL FINISH	L	PAVING SUBGRADE AND BASE COURSE	X	UTILITIES - SITE	KK
ELECTRICAL ROUGH-IN	M	PERMIT APPLICATION TIME	Y	WINDOWS AND DOORS	LL

LEGEND

CIRCLES WITH NUMBERS INSIDE ARE NODES REPRESENTING THE START AND FINISH OF EACH ACTIVITY.

A LETTER WITH A NUMBER UNDERNEATH REPRESENTS AN ACTIVITY AND ITS DURATION.

DASHED LINES HAVE NO TIME DURATION BUT SHOW THE RELATIONSHIP OF THE ACTIVITY TO OTHER WORK.

CONSTRUCTION ACTIVITY NETWORK

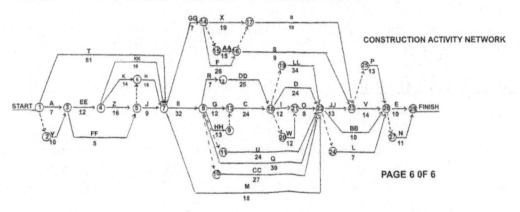

81

How to Read Blueprints - A Beginner's Guide

Before explaining how to read blueprints, it may be valuable to understand what blueprints are. It is quite difficult to build a structure to scale when the scale you are working with is very small. To make things a bit easier to read, architects and designers complete their drawings on large scale vellum sheets of various sizes. Probably the most common size for commercial work is 36" x 48".

Twenty years ago we didn't have the technology that we do today where most plans are drawn on computers by CAD systems. CAD is short for computer aided design. Plans were drawn by hand on semi-transparent film called vellum. Blueprints are then made by overlaying the vellum drawings on top of blueprint paper which is ran through the blueprint machine, which exposes the paper to intensified light and ammonia. This exposure to ammonia and light causes the blueprint paper to develop and the drawings are transposed in a dark blue color.

The vellum drawings were very valuable since it represented hours and hours of work that the architect put in to creating the drawing. But today the popular method for creating plans is by CAD. Once drawings are completed in the computer, they are plotted (printed) on a large-scale printer called a plotter. If the vellums are accidentally destroyed the architect has the plans on file to re-plot. Copies can now be made from these vellums by either a blueprint machine or a large scale printer for crisp "black and white" copies.

Typical blueprints will consist of the following pages, depending on the structure being built.
· Site Plan, also called the plot plan
· Elevations. Pictures of front, rear, left & right sides of building.
· Foundation plan. Shows footings, steel placement, etc.
· Floor plan. If there's more than one floor level, you will have multiple floor plans. Such as 2nd Floor, 3rd Floor, etc.
· Roof plan. This will show roof framing.
· Electrical plan. Placement of electrical service, switches, etc.
· HVAC & Plumbing plans.

Components of a blueprint or plan.

The Scale

Since plans cannot be the same size as the actual building, they have to be drawn small enough to fit on paper. The most common scale is ¼". This means that every ¼" equals 1 foot. A 1" line would equal 4 feet in our drawing. Larger buildings may be drawn in a smaller scale to get the building on the page. Each page of the plan will have the scale noted.   SCALE: ¼" = 1'

Dimension Lines

Measurements from one point to another are called dimension lines. These will be drawn as a solid line with a mark at either end. Different designers use different marks such as blocks or arrows.

Callouts or Call outs

You will probably notice a number of circles, triangles, or hexagons with numbers inside of them. Placed next to windows and doors and sometimes next to other elements such as lighting or plumbing fixtures, these notations correspond to those on the window, door, plumbing, and electrical schedules found elsewhere on the blueprint. These schedules indicate the size and types of the windows and doors to be used. Sometimes even the manufacturer and model numbers are on these schedules. They are a type of marker for us.

Schedules

In the previous section we mentioned the callouts would refer to the corresponding schedules; window, door, etc. To determine what window goes in the location shown here, we would check the callout and refer to the Window Schedule.

Cross Sections

Example of a Wall Section

A cross section is a "cut-away view" or "side view" of a particular portion of the building, showing us internal components of the building that are not visible or easy to draw on the plan from a "top view", such as a Floor Plan. Depending on the complexity of the building, there can be several of these on the blueprint. It will be important to the designer of the plan to express to the contractor every detail of the building. Many of these details are found within the wall section. There will be a larger scale used for the wall section.

Details

Areas of the building that the designer wants you to have a better understanding of are usually arranged on the Detail Page of the blueprints. If the building doesn't have enough details to warrant devoting an entire page to this endeavor, they will simply be put off to the side on the page where they are most relevant. The designer will mark the area of concern with a callout indicating which detail to refer to. This is a popular way for structural engineers to indicate details such as the type and size of straps, hangers, and nailing patterns.

Many of your tradesmen such as the Mason, Framer, Siding Contractor, Roofer, Drywall Contractor, and Insulation Contractor may need to refer to the same detail to define their work.

Windows and Doors

Openings in a building are placed and sized for many different reasons. The three main reasons would be for:
 Function
 Appearance
 Building Codes

A designer has to take all three into consideration when assembling the plan. The owner may want a door in a certain location, but this may interfere with the NC Accessibility Code or a Fire Code. Windows also have to meet certain egress codes (allowing for escape from fire) if they are in certain rooms and must be of a certain size and height from the floor.

Stairways

You will notice the "up arrow" indicating a stairway is going to the next level above this one and not downward to a lower level. There will also be details. The designer wants you to how this stairway is to be built.

Blueprint Pages

The following pages are the ones that are most typical in today's industry. Obviously, a blueprint for a multi-level industrial complex are going to be much more involved than those for a simple, single level retail store. But, we are working with the basics today.

Title Page

In general, this page contains the name and location of the project, the name of the architect and engineer and usually has an index to the drawings.

Site Plan

This plan is drawn to a different scale from the rest of the pages. As the site can be huge, a more common scale would be 1" = 20'. This would make it much easier to show the entire piece of property including property lines, just like a survey. The outline of the building will be placed on the plan with all the setback dimensions. Also, drives, walkways and parking lots will be on this page. Additional information that can be found on this page would be; elevations, benchmark, easements, and utility services such as water, electric etc...

Foundation Plan

Here you will find the dimensions of the building, the type of footers to support the building and the steel used for reinforcement. Your plumber and electrician will also use this page for locating plumbing waste lines and underground electrical. If there is a downdraft range and it is a floor is a slab on grade, your HVAC contractor will need to review this page and get his exhaust ductwork in place prior to pouring the floor slab.

Elevations

The elevation page will show the front, rear, left and right side of the building. Many of the details about the exterior materials and finish of the building will be on this page as well. Vertical dimensions will also be shown on this page.

Floor Plan

If you are building a one story building, then you will just have one of these. If your building has more than one story, there will be an additional page for the 2nd Floor. If there are more floors and they are identical, a page may read 2nd - 5th Floor. The Floor Plan is the most referred to page in the blueprint because it has the most information. Depending on the complexity of the interior, Floor Plans can be more diversified by separating the information onto two similar pages known as a Dimensional Floor Plan and an Architectural Floor Plan. The Dimensional Floor Plan will focus only on dimensions and there will be minimal or no text. The Architectural Floor Plan will have no dimensions, but many notes as to the names and descriptions of items that the designer feels are of importance.

The Floor Plan is where you will find the location of windows and doors, elevator shafts, Mechanical Rooms, stairways, plumbing fixtures, cabinetry, shelving, appliances and more.

Roof Plan

A complete drawing of how the roof is to be constructed will be found on this page. Framing members, steel decking notes, dimensions and specifications are all found here. If roof trusses are involved, a truss layout page will accompany this page for placement and bracing of the roof trusses.

Mechanicals

Your plan may also have additional pages for the trades. There will be an Electrical Page showing all the placement of lighting, switches, receptacles, electrical service and anything else needed to power the building. Another page is the HVAC Layout. This will show duct placement and sizes, air handler and condenser specifications and locations. The last would be a Plumbing Plan. This page will show supply lines, waste lines and their appropriate drops and angles and the size of pipe to use.

Detail Page

If a plan has many details, a separate page will be dedicated to this. This way, all of the details are gathered for ease of use.

In conclusion, we do hope this information was helpful to those needing a starting point. Learning to read blueprints is not something that happens overnight, but with exposure it is easy to catch on. The true task is finding information you are looking for where it should be on the plan. Don't be too surprised when you find conflicting information. This happens when owners make changes to plans in the beginning and the designer failed to correct all the pages affected. When the plans are not clear, consult with the designer for clarification. This is much less expensive than the alternative.

Contract Administration
Practice Exam #1

For Questions 1 through 4, refer to Plan Set #9501

1. On sheet 2 of 15 of plan set #9501, the distance from gridline point D1 to gridline point D12 is _____ ft.

    A. 18
    B. 134
    C. 136
    D. 140

2. Drawing detail ①/④ and general note 17 on Sheet 3 of 15 show the construction details for all interior partition walls. A total of _____ lineal feet of these partition walls is going to be installed on this project.

    A. 119
    B. 144
    C. 187
    D. 178

3. _____ cubic yards of concrete are required to pour all the foundation footings marked as #5 locations. Do not deduct for the volume of any steel reinforcing. Select the closest answer.

    A. 5
    B. 10
    C. 15
    D. 20

4. _____ 18H5 bar joists are required for the project's main tower roof framing.

    A. 24
    B. 30
    C. 42
    D. 54

Use the following site plan to answer questions 5 and 6. The angle at point A = the angle at point C = 90 °.

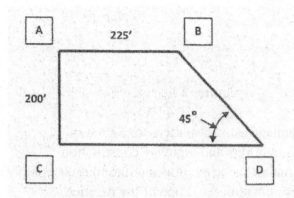

5. The distance from point B to point C on the plan is _____ ft.

    A. 301.04
    B. 282.84
    C. 318.19
    D. 425

6. The Owner wants to install sod on his property. The contractor will order _____ square foot of sod for his property. Select the closest answer.

    A. 45,000
    B. 50,000
    C. 55,000
    D. 65,000

7. The total Labor and Material cost for a project was estimated to be $250,000 and 55% of that total was estimated for Materials. The additional profit on the job will be _____ if actual Labor costs were only 85% of the estimated Labor costs.

    A. $14,965
    B. $16,875
    C. $18,402
    D. More than $20,000

8.Temporary structures shall have an exit access travel distance of _____ feet or less.

    A. 120
    B. 100
    C. 180
    D. 75

9. Ownership passes to the company at the point where the goods are FOB or _____.

    A. First on board
    B. Free on board
    C. Freight on board
    D. Final on board

10. In the state of Florida, _____ requires a license.

    A. A contractor repairing damaged storm shutters for $1500.
    B. A contractor specializing in bridge and highway construction.
    C. A University of Florida maintenance employee doing routine repairs not exceeding $200,000.
    D. A registered architect acting within the scope of her practice.

11. The first offense by a person falsely presenting themselves as a licensed contractor is a _____.

    A. First degree felony
    B. Second degree misdemeanor
    C. Third degree felony
    D. First degree misdemeanor

12. In a threshold building, the contractor's contractual or statutory obligations shall not be relieved _____.

    A. By decisions rendered by the building official
    B. By any action of the special inspector
    C. By any mutual agreement between the special inspector and the owner
    D. By the engineer or architect of record

13. The burden of proof of the merit of any proposed substitution is upon the _____.

    A. Architect
    B. Contractor
    C. Proposer
    D. Initial Decision Maker

14. A(an) _____ warranty work in construction would be used for its intended purpose.

    A. Contingent
    B. Expressed
    C. Implied
    D. Conditional

15. If the Subcontractor fails within _____ days after receipt of written notice from the Contractor to correct defective Work, the Contractor may make good such deficiencies.

    A. Five calendar
    B. Seven working
    C. Five working
    D. Seven calendar

16. The Architect will _____ after receipt of a Contractor's Application for Payment, either issue to the Owner a Certificate for Payment or notify the Contractor and Owner in writing of the Architect's reasons for withholding certification.

    A. Within seven working days
    B. Within seven days
    C. At least ten calendar days
    D. Promptly

17. According to the Davis-Bacon Act, the _____ may withhold contract payments to cover alleged under-payments of wages.

    A. State
    B. Architect
    C. Local municipal
    D. Secretary of Labor

18. If you are not in direct privity of contract with the owner, the Construction Lien Law requires that you _____.

    A. Serve a notice to owner
    B. Do not have to service a notice to owner
    C. Have to get releases
    D. Do not have to get releases

19. If a #2 framing lumber is selling for $6.50 per board-foot, the cost of 820 lineal feet of 2x4, 686 lineal feet of 2x6 and 243 lineal feet of 2x8 would be _____. Select the closest answer.

    A. $9,960
    B. $10,120
    C. $12,260
    D. $14,440

20. Building inspections shall include _____.

    A. Framing, Roofing, Mechanical, Electrical and Plumbing inspections
    B. Foundation, Framing, Roofing, Electrical and Plumbing inspections
    C. Foundation, Framing, Sheathing, Roofing and Final inspections
    D. Foundation, Framing, Gas and Swimming Pool inspections

21. Temporary sanitary facilities and drinking water are typically covered by the _____ of a contract.

    A. General Conditions
    B. Supplementary General Conditions
    C. Specifications
    D. Miscellaneous Contract Conditions

22. _____ limit is NOT one the limits of liability under a Commercial General Liability insurance policy.

    A. General aggregate
    B. Medical expense
    C. Property damage during construction
    D. Personal advertising

23. A Contractor submitted an application for a progress payment. The project has a $246,000 contract amount and was 66% complete at the time of the payment application. The Architect did not certify $22,000 of the requested amount. The retainage rate is 10%. The Contractor should expect to receive _____. Select the closest answer.

    A. $167,300
    B. $126,325
    C. $162,360
    D. $146,124

24. Change Orders with back charges to the Contractor when the Owner corrects defective work shall include _____ costs of correcting such deficiencies.

    A. Actual
    B. Probable
    C. Negotiated
    D. Reasonable

25. A permanent sign identifying the termite treatment provider and need for reinspection and treatment contract renewal shall be provided and posted near the _____.

    A. Water heater or electrical panel
    B. Garage entry door
    C. Control panel
    D. Air handler unit

26. Because inventory is consumed over a relatively short period of time, usually not exceeding one year, it is regarded as a _____ of a company.

    A. Current liability
    B. Recurring expense
    C. Current asset
    D. Miscellaneous item

27. _____ is an example of work that does NOT require a building permit.

    A. Adding a patio door to an existing home
    B. Repairing a storm-damaged roof
    C. Reroofing an existing home without removing the existing shingles
    D. Installing portable ventilation equipment

28. Addenda are modifications to or interpretations of the Bidding Documents and will be issued _____.

    A. No later than four days from the date for receipt of Bids
    B. Prior to the date for the receipt of Bids
    C. No sooner than two days prior to the date for the receipt of Bids
    D. No later than four days prior to the date for receipt of Bids

29. Construction materials and equipment shall not be placed or stored within _____ feet of a street intersection.

    A. 10
    B. 15
    C. 20
    D. 25

30. In general, a contract _____ should be recognized as complete under the completed contract method.

    A. That is complete except for retainage
    B. That is 100% complete
    C. That is 95% to 100% completed
    D. In excess of 98% or 99% completed

31. All employers with _____ employee(s) must maintain an OSHA 300/300A log.

    A. Two
    B. Eight
    C. Ten
    D. Eleven

32. In network construction, _____ are those which are based upon physical characteristics of the work and is normally inflexible.

    A. Unforeseen events
    B. Practical considerations of policy
    C. Hard dependencies
    D. Soft dependencies

33. It is estimated that the Contractor will need to purchase 250 2 x 4's that are only available in 10 ft lengths. If the lumber yard pricing per board foot is $6.50 and sales tax is 7%, the amount to be budgeted should be _____. Select the closest answer.

    A. $10,900
    B. $11,000
    C. $11,200
    D. $11,600

34. Among the State requirements for educational facilities is the requirement that new buildings, additions, renovations and remodeling shall not be occupied until the building has received a (n) _____.

    A. Certificate of completion from the Architect
    B. Notice of compliance from the State Fire Marshall
    C. Certificate of occupancy
    D. State Acceptance Certificate

35. The Contractor shall NOT be responsible for _____.

    A. Initiating all safety precautions and programs
    B. Maintaining all safety precautions and programs
    C. Scheduling safety compliance inspections
    D. Supervising all safety precautions and programs

36. _____ are NOT items that are included in the general conditions of a contract.

    A. Correction of work and coordination of work
    B. Jobsite offices
    C. Compliance with all laws and regulations and insurance
    D. Shop drawings

37. A Subcontractor may terminate a Subcontract for nonpayment of amounts due for_____ days or longer.

    A. 10
    B. 30
    C. 60
    D. 45

38. Alterations made to provide an accessible path of travel to the altered area will be deemed disproportionate to the overall alteration when the cost exceeds _____ percent.

    A. 10
    B. 15
    C. 20
    D. 25

39. An accurate estimating method that lists all materials and labor needed for an element of work or project is called _____ method.

    A. Detailed survey or piece
    B. Unit price
    C. Square footage
    D. Guaranteed maximum price

40. Under the legal principal of _____, a contractor may be entitled to a reasonable value of the work requested and performed even without reaching an agreement.

    A. Nolo contendere
    B. Quantum meriut
    C. Waiver of consequential damages
    D. Principal of Indemnity

41. Under FL Lien Law, a person who knowingly uses funds paid on account of a $950 project without paying subs, suppliers and/or laborers is guilty of misapplication of construction funds has committed a _____.

    A. First degree misdemeanor
    B. Felony
    C. Felony of the second degree
    D. Felony of the third degree

42. Walkways for pedestrians in front of demolition projects during the renovation of an existing building shall be of sufficient width to accommodate pedestrian traffic but in no case shall _____.

    A. Be protected by barricades not less than 6 feet in height
    B. Be a minimum of 42 inches in width
    C. Be designed to a minimum live load of 150 psf
    D. Not be less than 4 feet in width

43. The _____ method is the simplest method of accounting control of inventory.

    A. First in, first out
    B. Last in, first out
    C. Item by item
    D. Average cost

44. A _____ clause is typically found in subcontract agreements between the contractor and subcontractor.

    A. Merger
    B. Dispute resolution
    C. Flow down
    D. Bond

45. The injured worker has _____ days in which to advise the employer of the fact that an accident has occurred.

    A. Seven
    B. Fourteen
    C. Twenty-one
    D. Thirty

46. The date for receipt of bids for a project is Friday, Oct 9. The last date on which Addenda modifying the bid documents may be issued is _____.

    A. Saturday, Oct 3
    B. Sunday, Oct 4
    C. Monday, Oct 5
    D. Tuesday, Oct 6

47. The fee owner of a threshold building shall select and pay all the costs of employing a special inspector, but the special inspector shall be responsible to _____.

    A. The enforcement agency
    B. The Contractor
    C. The Architect
    D. The Owner

48. The _____ owns the drawings for a completed project.

    A. The Architect
    B. The Owner
    C. The Contractor
    D. None of the above

49. A concrete slab 140'-8" long, 75'-10" wide and 9-1 /2" thick will require _____ cubic yards of concrete. Select the closest answer.

    A. Between 200 and 250
    B. Between 250 and 275
    C. Between 275 and 300
    D. Between 300 and 325

50. An application for a permit for any proposed work shall be deemed to have been abandoned _____ days after date of filing.

    A. 30
    B. 45
    C. 90
    D. 180

51. A _____ bond exempts the owner's real property from claims of lien.

    A. Fidelity
    B. Payment
    C. Lien transfer
    D. Maintenance

52. The Subcontractor shall furnish the Contractor periodic progress reports _____ on the Work of this Subcontract.

    A. Weekly
    B. At the time of each application for payment
    C. As mutually agreed
    D. Upon demand

53. In cases of Claims for additional time due to a continuing delay, _____.

    A. The Contractor must resubmit his Claim weekly for each week the delay continues
    B. The allowance for additional time is capped at four weeks
    C. Only one Claim is necessary to be filed
    D. The Claim must be mediated before going to binding arbitration

54. Construction lien law is NOT applicable to _____.

    A. Condominiums
    B. Public property
    C. Leasehold property
    D. Property owned by married persons

55. General Contractor license holders are NOT required to subcontract _____.

    A. Electrical work on new buildings of their own construction
    B. HVAC work
    C. The installation of wood shingles, wood shakes, or asphalt or fiberglass shingle roofing on new buildings of their own construction
    D. Swimming pool finish work

56. The construction manager contracts and acts as agent for the owner in a _____ contract.

    A. Construction management contract
    B. Competitive bid contract
    C. Cost-plus contract
    D. Time and materials contract

57. The maximum fine to be imposed on a contractor for working with a delinquent license and it is a second offense would be _____ .

    A. 1,500
    B. 2,500
    C. 3,000
    D. 5,000

58. Trusses on a new, single-family detached residential project, shall be inspected _____.

    A. By the building official during the framing inspection
    B. By the building official during the roofing inspection
    C. By the building official during the sheathing inspection
    D. By a 3rd party registered design professional at the project site after installation by the contractor

59. Allowances do NOT include _____.

    A. The Contractor's costs for unloading and handling
    B. The Contractor's cost of equipment delivered
    C. The Contractor's cost of materials delivered
    D. Applicable trade discounts

60. Any required certificates of inspection shall be secured by the _____.

    A. Owner
    B. Architect
    C. Contractor
    D. Building Official

51. The cost to backfill and compact a 15 ft x 25 ft x 5 ft deep excavation with vertical sides if the excavation contractor charges $1.75 per square foot for each 6-inch lift is_____. Select the closest answer.

    A. $3,750
    B. $8,200
    C. $6,565
    D. $7,875

52. An approved water supply for fire protection shall be made available _____.

    A. As soon as combustible material arrives on the site
    B. Before construction begins at the site
    C. At a time determined by the Building Official
    D. At a time determined by the Fire Marshal

53. Requests for clarification or interpretation of the Bidding Documents shall reach the Architect at least _____ days prior to the date for receipt of Bids.

    A. Three
    B. Seven
    C Four
    D. Ten

54. An employee who feels they have been discriminated against because they reported a suspected OSHA violation may file a complaint with the nearest OSHA office within _____ days of this alleged discrimination.

    A. 30
    B. 45
    C. 90
    D. 180

55. In the contract provisions, insurance to be maintained by contractor will be specified in the _____.

    A. Proposal
    B. General conditions
    C. Supplementary general conditions
    D. Special conditions and requirements

Please See Answer Key on following page
ALH 02/10/2022

97

1 Exam Prep
Contract Administration
Practice Exam #1 Answers

The following abbreviations are used in the Table below:

CM: Florida Contractors Manual
BGTA: Builders Guide to Accounting, 2001
A201, A401, A701: Various AIA documents
FBC: FL Building Code; Building/Residential/Existing Building/Energy
Conservation/ Accessibility
Walker's: Walker's Building Estimator's Reference Book
OSHA: 29 CFR 1926 OSHA Construction Industry Regulations
PPCC: Principles and Practices of Commercial Construction
DCCM: Design and Control of Concrete Mixtures
Rebar: Placing Reinforcing Bars
Gypsum: Application and Finishing of Gypsum Panel Products, GA-216
EEBC: Energy Efficient Building Construction in Florida
Truss: BCSI Guide to Good Practice for handling, Installing, Restraining & Bracing of
Metal Plate Connected Wood Trusses
TOC: Table of Contents

Question Answer Location (search hints in parentheses)

No.	Answer	Location
1	B	Sheet 2/15 Foundation Plan – add all or take total length minus 1 ft each side – 136 ft – 2 ft = 134ft
2	C	Sheet 3/15, Note 17: Column boxing, 1' Typical Each partition wall is 18 feet less 6 inches at each end for column boxing. Net lineal footage per wall= 17 ft. Sheet 3 shows 1 partition wall on the 1st Floor Plan. Sheet 4 shows 2 partition walls on the 2nd Floor Plan. Sheet 5 shows 4 partition walls on BOTH the 3rd and 4th Floor Plans for a total of 8. Total number of walls = 1+2+8 = 11 x 17 ft/wall = 187 ft
3	D	Sheet 10/15 Column and Footing Schedule At each #5 location, volume of concrete= 8.5 ft x 9.5 ft x 1.67 ft =134.85 cft There are 4 locations marked as #5 on sheet 2/15 Foundation Plan 4 x 134.85 cft = 539.4 cft / 27 cft/cyd= 19.98 cyd
4	D	Sheet 13/15 Roof Framing Plan – 12 + 12 + 6 + 9 + 9 + 6 = 54
5	A	Right triangle – Pythagorean Theorem – (Line AC)^2 + (Line AB)^2 = (Line BC)^2 so Line BC is equal to the square root of $\sqrt{200^2 + 225^2} = \sqrt{40,000+50,625} = 301.04$ ft
6	D	Add areas together – rectangle = 200 ft x 225 ft = 45,000 sqft – Since you know that one leg of 45° triangle is 200 ft, then the other leg is also 200ft Triangle area = ½ (200 ft x 200 ft) = 20,000 sqft Net area= 45,000 sqft + 20,000 sqft = 65,000 sqft

7	B	100% -55% for materials = 45% of total estimated for Labor $250,000 x 45%= $112,500 (original ESTIMATED Labor cost). $112,500 x 85%= $95,625 (ACTUAL Labor cost). $112,500 - $95,625 = $16,875 additional profit.
8	B	FBC- Building, sect. 3103.4 (Index: "Temporary Structures –Means of egress")
9	B	CM, pg. 3-58 (Index: "Inventory")
10	A	CM, 2021 pg. 2-18; 2017 pg. 2-6 (Index: "Licensing – Exemptions")
11	D	CM, 2021 pg. 2-29; 2017 pg. 2-14 (Index: "Penalties, Unlicensed Activity")
12	B	FBC-Building, sect. 110.8.1 – Place tab for Threshold
13	C	AIA A701, art. 3.3.3 – (TOC: "Chapter 3 – Bidding Documents")
14	C	CM, pg. 8-10 (Index: "Contracts – Warranties")
15	C	AIA A401, art. 3.5 - (TOC: "Chapter 3 - Contractor")
16	B	AIA A201, art. 9.4.1 (Index: Certificate of Payment)
17	D	CM, pg. 5-33 (Index: "Acts – Davis Bacon")
18	A	CM, 2021 9-20 to 9-22; 2017 pg. 9-19 to 9-21 (Index: "Liens – Privity")
19	B	Board-foot formula: Walker's, (32nd Ed.) Pg. 376 (31st Ed.) Pg. 633 (2 x 4 x 820) ÷ 12 = 546.67 bdft (2 x 6 x 686) ÷12 = 686 bdft (2 x 8 x 243) ÷12 =324 bdft 546.67 + 686 + 324 =1,556.67 bdft x $6.50/bdft = $10,118.40
20	C	FBC-Building, sect. 110.3 (Index: "Inspections, Required")
21	B	CM, pg. 10-11 (Index: "Contracts – see Contract Clauses – General Conditions")
22	C	CM, pg. 4-8 (Index: "Insurance - Business Liability")
23	B	$246,000 x 66%= $162,360. The Architect did not certify $22,000. $162,360- $22,000= $140,360. The retainage rate is 10%. So, the amount that would be paid would be $140,360 - 10% ($140,360) = $126,324 or $140,360 x .90 = $126,324
24	D	AIA A201, art. 2.5 (Index: "Owners Right to Carry Out the Work")
25	A	FBC-Building, sect. 105.11 (Index: "Inspections")
26	C	CM, pg. 3-58. (Index: "Inventory" and TOC: Chap 3 "Inventory Accounting")
27	D	FBC-Building, sect. 105.2 (Index: "Permits")
28	D	AIA A701, art. 3.4.3. (Index: "Addenda")
29	C	FBC-Building, sect. 3308.1.1 (Index: "Safeguards During Construction – Temporary use of streets, alleys and public property")
30	D	CM, pg. 3-80 (Index: "Completed Contract")
31	D	CM, pg. 7-6 (Index: "OSHA – Responsibilities")
32	C	CM, pgs. 10-57 thru 10-59 (Index: "Network Analysis Technique" and "Scheduling – Network Analysis")
33	D	Walker's, (32nd Ed.) Pg. 376 (31st Ed.) Pg. 633 Board Feet = Width (inches) x Thickness (inches) x Length (feet) / 12 2 x 4 x 10 ÷ 12 = 6.6667 x 250 = 1666.67 bdft x $6.50 per board feet = $10,833.35 x 1.07 sales tax = $11,591.68 round up to $11,600.00
34	C	FBC-Building, sect. 453.3.7 (TOC: Chap 4 "State Requirements for Educational Facilities")

35	C	AIA A201, art. 10.1 (Index: "Safety Precautions and Programs")
36	B	CM, pg. 10-10 (Index: "Contract Clauses – General Conditions")
37	C	AIA A401, art. 7.1. (TOC: "Termination, Suspension or Assignment of the Subcontract")
38	C	FBC-Accessibility, sect. 202.4.1 (TOC: "Existing Buildings and Facilities")
39	A	CM, pg. 10-12 (Index: "Types of Estimates")
40	B	CM, pg. 8-6 (Index: "Contracts – Written or Oral or Quantum Meriut")
41	D	CM, 2021 pg. 9-42; 2017 pg. 9-41. (TOC: Chap. 9 "Misapplication of Construction Funds") and Statute 713.345(1)(b)(3) CM, 2021 pg. 9-93 and 2017 pg. 9-120.
42	D	FBC-Building, sect. 3306.2 pg. (Index: "Walkway, During construction" and TOC: Chap 33 "Safeguards During Construction - Protection of Pedestrians)
43	D	CM, pg. 3-59 (Index: "Inventory")
44	C	CM, pg. 8-15 (Index: "Contract – Contract Clauses – see Contract Clauses – Flow down")
45	D	CM, pg. 6-11 (Index: "Workers Compensation – After the Accident")
46	B	AIA A701, art. 3.4.3 (TOC: "Chapter 3 – Bidding Documents")
47	A	FBC-Building, sect. 110.8.3 TAB – Threshold
48	A	AIA A201, art 1.5.1. (Index: "Ownership and Use of Drawings, Specifications and Other Instruments of Service")
49	D	140.67 ft x 75.83 ft x (9.5/12) ft= 8,444.71 cft – convert to cyd– 8,444.71 cft / 27 cft per cyd= 312.76 cyd Trade Knowledge
50	D	FBC-Building, sect. 105.3.2 (Index: "Permits - Time Limitations")
51	B	CM, 2021 pg. 9-57; 2017 pg. 9-56 (Index: "Bonds – Payment Bonds")
52	C	AIA A401, art. 4.2.4 (TOC: "Chapter 4 - Subcontractors")
53	C	AIA A201, art 15.1.6.1. (Index: "Claims for Additional Time")
54	B	CM, 2021 pg. 9-11; 2017 pg. 9-10 (Index: "Liens – Exemptions")
55	C	CM, 2021 pg. 2-20; 2017 pg. 2-7 (Index: "Licensing – Subcontracting Requirements")
56	A	CM, pg. 8-8 (Index: "Types of Contracts")
57	D	CM, 2017 pg. 2-185 and 2021 pg. 2-158 / 61G4-17 (Index: "Licensing - Penalties")
58	A	FBC-Building, sect. 110.3 (Index: "Inspections, Required")
59	D	AIA A201, art. 3.8.2 (Index: "Allowances")
60	C	AIA A201, art. 13.4.4 (Index: "Certificates of Inspection, Testing or Approval")
61	C	Cost for each "lift" =15 ft x 25 ft= 375 sf x $1.75/sf = $656.25 per lift Number of 6" lifts= 5 ft deep ÷ .5 ft per lift= 10 lifts Total cost to backfill and compact= $656.25 x 10= $6,562.50
62	A	FBC-Building, sect. [F] 3313.1 (Index: "Safeguards During Construction" and TOC: Chap 33 "Safeguards During Construction- Water Supply for Fire Protection)
63	B	AIA A701, art. 3.2.2. (TOC: "Bidding Documents")
64	A	CM, pg.7-31 (Index: "Penalties – OSHA Civil")
65	B	CM, pg.10-10 (TOC: "Chap 10 Plans and Specifications - Agreement")

Contract Administration
Practice Exam #2

*** *For Questions 1 through 4, refer to Plan Set #9501* ***

1. The foundation footers marked with the grid point C5 will require _____ cubic yards to pour. Select the closet answer.

    A. 20
    B. 22
    C. 26
    D. 28

2. _____ inches of compacted limerock are to be placed beneath the asphalt surface of all parking areas.

    A. 1 1/2
    B. 2
    C. 5
    D. 6

3. _____ measured in-place cubic yards of topsoil are required for the planters if the topsoil layer is 10 inches deep. Select the closet answer.

    A. 1.00
    B. 2.00
    C. 2.10
    D. 3.05

4. This project will require _____ lineal feet of fencing to enclose the property. There are three (3) 8 ft gates to be installed. Select the closet answer.

    A. 1,231
    B. 1,429
    C. 1,462
    D. 1,485

Use the following site plan to answer questions 5 and 6. In this site plan, the following facts are known:

• The angle at point C = the angle at point D = 45°
• The distance from point A to point B = 75 yards (yds)

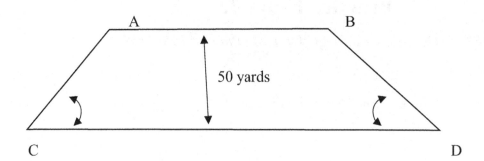

5. The distance from point C to point D is _____ yds.

    A. 100
    B. 125
    C. 150
    D. 175

6. A fencing contractor is invited to submit a bid to enclose the entire site in 6' construction site security fencing. If the contractor charges $12 per running foot for such fencing, his bid pricing will be _____. Select the closest answer.

    A. $ 5,000
    B. $14,000
    C. $18,000
    D. More than $20,000

7. The Job Status Report, which indicates the percentage completed by each major construction activity, is completed by the _____.

    A. Project Engineer or Owner
    B. Project Engineer or Field Superintendent
    C. Project Engineer or Project Manager
    D. Project Engineer or Architect.

8. A demolition first inspection shall be made _____ .

    A. Before all utility connections have been disconnected
    B. After all utility connections have been disconnected
    C. Before all utility connections have been capped off
    D. After all utility connections have been capped off

9. A contractor wins a job for a low bid of $120,000. If his total costs and expenses are $90,000, his margin of profit is _____ %.

    A. 25
    B. 33
    C. 75
    D. 133

10. A proposal is a legal instrument that will NOT bind the Contractor to the Owner if _____.

    A. The proposal form is filled out properly and completely.
    B. The contractor forfeits the bid bond.
    C. The contractor does not forfeit the bid bond.
    D. The owner/prime contractor accepts the proposal.

11. Submittal documents shall be submitted in _____ or more sets with each permit application.

    A. 1
    B. 2
    C. 3
    D. 4

12. A business's_____ insurance shall apply if property damages caused by construction are experienced at a project after all work on the project has been completed and put to its intended use.

    A. Builder's Risk
    B. General Liability
    C. Installation Floater
    D. Fidelity Bond

13. Nightclubs and restaurants are classified as Group _____ occupancies.

    A. A-1
    B. A-2
    C. B
    D. M

14. A (The)_____ is (are) NOT required for a minimum plan review prior to building permitting by the building official.

    A. Foundation plan
    B. Plumbing elevations
    C. Rear elevation
    D. Roof framing plan

15._____ is (are) NOT required to be stored at the construction site by the Contractor.

    A. Drawings
    B. Shop drawings
    C. Change orders
    D. Material invoices

16. A general, building, or residential contractor is NOT required to subcontract the installation of wood shingles, wood shakes, or asphalt or fiberglass shingle roofing materials_____.

    A. On new buildings of their own construction
    B. On an existing roof that needs repair
    C. When permitting requirements have been satisfied
    D. On all roofs

17. A Notice of Commencement has not been filed on a $10,000 project. The initial indication of a problem will be that the Contractor is unable to get _____.

    A. The first building inspection
    B. Final payment from owner
    C. A Certificate of Occupancy
    D. A final inspection

18. _____ is a non-operable fenestration unit primarily designed to transmit daylight from a roof surface to an interior ceiling.

    A. Tubular Daylighting Device (TDD)
    B. Tubular Fenestration Device (TFD)
    C. Tubular Lighting Device (TLD)
    D. Tubular Device (TD)

19. The vertical clearance from the public right-of-way to the lowest part of any awning shall be not less than _____ feet.

    A. 7
    B. 8
    C. 2
    D. 15

20. One set of approved construction documents shall be retained by the building official for a period of not less than _____ days from date of completion of the permitted work.

    A. 90
    B. 120
    C. 180
    D. 210

21. If there are multiple liens on a project, only a limited amount of funds to pay the liens, and all liens were filed at the same time, _____ would be paid first.

    A. Liens of laborers
    B. Liens of the contractor
    C. Liens of the supplier
    D. All liens except those of the supplier

22. The _____ is authorized to issue a stop work order.

    A. Owner's representative
    B. Building inspector
    C. Building official
    D. Special inspector

23. _____ the company is in charge of the safety program.

    A. The owner of
    B. The safety manager employed by
    C. The contractor who qualifies
    D. One person within

24. Installing a/an _____ does NOT require a permit.

    A. screen enclosure
    B. elevator
    C. cell tower
    D. portable cooling unit

25. A permit from the _____ is required prior to the start of construction of a habitable structure that is seaward to a coastal control line.

    A. Building Department
    B. Florida Department of Environmental Protection
    C. Army Core of Engineers
    D. South Florida Water Management

26. _____ is true regarding Surety Bonding.

    A. It is a two-party agreement between the individual and the insurance company
    B. Losses are not contemplated
    C. The law of large numbers is used to determine the premium
    D. The surety will spread losses among policyholders

27. When developing a schedule using a Project Logic Table, _____ should NOT be considered.

    A. Crew size
    B. Activities
    C. Manpower Levels
    D. A and C

28. A general "rule of thumb" for calculating the bonding capacity of a contractor is to determine the net quick and multiply it by a factor of _____.

    A. 2
    B. 5
    C. 10
    D. 20

29. _____ would result in disciplinary action by the licensing board.

    A. Not applying for a certificate of authority

    B. Relying on a building code interpretation rendered by a building official

    C. Intimidating, threatening, coercing, or otherwise discouraging the service of a notice to owner or a notice to contractor

    D. Abandoning the project after 30 days, or failure to perform work without just cause for 30 consecutive days

30. Prior to the settlement of an insured loss, the Owner shall notify the Contractor of terms and the Contractor shall have _____ days from the receipt of notice to object to the proposed settlement or allocation of the proceeds.

    A. 3

    B. 5

    C. 10

    D. 14

31. If a contractor paid $3,875 for supplies which included 7% sales tax, the cost of the supplies without the sales tax was _____. Select the closest answer.

    A. $3,625

    B. $3,555

    C. $3,622

    D. $3,526

32. CSI MasterFormat divides specifications into _____ specific divisions.

    A. 48

    B. 49

    C. 50

    D. 51

33. Regarding certification of registered contractors, which of the following is NOT a requirement a contractor must meet for grandfathering?

    A. Is in compliance with the insurance and financial responsibility requirements in Florida Statue 489.115 (5)

    B. Has at least 6 years of active, probation experience in that contracting category

    C. Has, for that contracting category, passed a written examination that the board finds to be substantially   similar to the examination required to be licensed as a certified contractor

    D. Has not had his or her contractor's license suspended or been assessed a fine in excess of $500 within the last   5 years

34. If the Contractor encounters concealed physical conditions that differ material from those indicated in the Contract Documents, he shall provide prompt notice to the Owner and Architect no later than ____.

    A. 14 days after the Owner has observed the conditions

    B. 14 days after observance by Contractor

    C. 14 days after first observance by Contractor

    D. 14 days after the Architect has observed the conditions

35. The difference between the cash received and the principal due at the end of a discount loan is known as the _____.

    A. Discount
    B. Compound interest
    C. Maturity value
    D. Installment

36. A building demolition specialty contractor is a contractor who has the skill to demolish structures _____ ft or less in height.

    A. 10
    B. 20
    C. 50
    D. 100

37. _____ need (s) to have a license in the State of Florida to do construction/contracting work.

    A. Liquified petroleum gas dealers
    B. A handyman who has a $1,500 project
    C. A person installing or maintaining fire suppression equipment
    D. A person who installs or maintains water conditioning units

38. A person who willfully files a fraudulent lien is guilty of a _____.

    A. Second degree misdemeanor
    B. First degree felony
    C. Second degree felony
    D. Third degree felony

39. Failure to furnish a sworn statement within _____ days shall result in the loss of lien rights.

    A. 30
    B. 45
    C. 60
    D. 90

40. The contractor must, within _____ days after receipt of the owner's written request, furnish to the property owner or his representative a list of the subcontractors and suppliers that were used on the project.

    A. 5
    B. 10
    C. 14
    D. 21

41. The Architect will prepare a Construction Change Directive _____.

    A. When there is no change to the contract time or cost
    B. In the absence of total agreement on the terms of a Change Order
    C. Only when the contractor agrees
    D. When there is no time to create a Change Order

42. Long lead items should be _____.

    A. Identified and ordered early
    B. Over stocked for emergency use
    C. Classified as shelf Items
    D. Ordered at same time as other materials

43. EPA asbestos regulations for demolition of commercial, industrial, and publicly owned buildings and residential structures with four or more dwelling units require a notification be sent to the Florida Department of Environmental Protection _____.

    A. At least 7 days before beginning the demolition
    B. At least 7 working days before beginning the demolition
    C. At least 10 days before beginning the demolition
    D. At least 10 working days before beginning the demolition

44. The Construction Change Directive when prepared does not have to be signed by the _____.

    A. Contractor
    B. Owner
    C. Architect
    D. B and C

45. The log and summary, OSHA No. 300/300A, should be kept for _____ calendar years following the end of the year to which they relate.

    A. 3
    B. 4
    C. 5
    D. 6

46. If the Initial Decision Maker requests a party to provide a response to a Claim or to furnish additional supporting data, such party shall respond within _____ days after receipt of such request.

    A. 60
    B. 30
    C. 21
    D. 10

47. The Florida Civil Rights Act of 1992 (FCRA) does NOT prohibit employment discrimination based on_____.

    A. Age
    B. Alcoholism
    C. Drug Abuse
    D. Religion

48. An Installation Floater is an insurance policy that covers _____.

    A. Subcontractor materials in transit
    B. Subcontractors business liability
    C. Umbrella liability
    D. Valuable papers and records

49. _____ is the minimum fine to be cited by OSHA for a willful serious penalty.

    A. $ 9,639
    B. $12,471
    C. $49,884
    D. $124,709

50. A contractor is hired to paint a stucco wall. The wall is 3000 ft long by 10 ft high and contains 20 windows that measure 3 ft x 4 ft. The painter can apply paint at the rate of 200 sqft per hour. The total Labor cost for this project will be _____if the painter charges $25 per hour and the job requires two (2) coats.

    A. $7,400 to $7,449
    B. $7,450 to $7,499
    C. Less than $7,400
    D. More than $7,500

51. The total Labor and Materials cost for a project was estimated to be $266,000 and 55% was estimated for Materials. The additional profit on this project will be _____ if the actual Labor costs were 85% of the originally estimated Labor costs.

    A. $11,970
    B. $17,955
    C. $21,945
    D. $39,900

52. In a precedence diagram, lines linking the boxes are called _____.

    A. Activities
    B. Connectors
    C. Arrow networks
    D. Dependences

53. Fictitious names are valid for _____ years.

    A. 3
    B. 4
    C. 5
    D. 6

54. _____ are employers that are NOT exempt from the broad coverage of OSHA.

    A. Religious establishments
    B. Employers of household workers
    C. Airport convenience stores
    D. Individuals that do not have "employees"

55. The _____ ACT protects covered employees against retaliation for participation in an investigation, hearing or for refusing to violate the law.

    A. Taft Hartley
    B. Public Whistle-blowers
    C. Williams-Steiger
    D. Portal to Portal

56. A secondary qualifying agent is responsible for _____.

    A. The supervision of fieldwork at sites where his/her license was used to obtain the building permit
    B. Any work for which he/she accepts responsibility
    C. Supervision of financial matters
    D. A and B but not C

57. A contract was signed by all parties on July 1, 2018. The date of commencement was given as July 9, 2018. If the work in the contract is to take 18 days, the date of substantial completion should be _____.

    A. July 26, 2018
    B. July 27, 2018
    C. July 28, 2018
    D. July 29, 2018

58. _____in any action against an unlicensed contractor for injuries sustained resulting from the contractor's negligence, malfeasance or misfeasance.

    A. The consumer is entitled to two times the actual damages sustained, plus costs and plus attorney's fees.
    B. The consumer is entitled to 1-1 /2 times the actual damages sustained, plus costs and plus attorney's fees.
    C. The contractor will pay a fine of $1,000 or 10% of the cost, whichever is greater.
    D. The consumer is entitled to three times the actual damages sustained, plus costs and attorney's fees.

59. The _____ shall not permit any part of the construction or site to be loaded so as to cause damage or create an unsafe condition.

    A. OSHA Inspector
    B. Owner
    C. Contractor
    D. Subcontractor

60. If you pay an independent contractor at least $600, it is your responsibility to _____.

    A. File a 1099
    B. Provide a contract
    C. File a W-2
    D. File a W-4

61. Movable fabric awnings or fabric covered frames may extend over public property for a distance of not more than _____ feet.

    A. 3
    B. 5
    C. 7
    D. 8

62. _____ does NOT need to be written to be enforceable.

    A. An agreement for a construction project with a two-year duration
    B. An agreement for a five-year lease
    C. An agreement to guaranty the debt of another
    D. An agreement for the sale of goods less than $500

63. _____ for latent defects discovered on a project.

    A. The contractor is liable for one year.
    B. The contractor's liability is restricted to claims by the first owner.
    C. The contractor is liable for the entire warranty period.
    D. The contractor's liability is subject to the statute of limitations.

64. A project requires 388,000 lbs. of steel beams and columns. Delivery charges this year are 7% greater than last year. _____ will be the total additional delivery charge if last year's delivery charge was $65.00 per ton. Select the closest answer.

    A. $70.00
    B. $13,500
    C. $950.00
    D. $885.00

65. The _____ shall directly arrange and pay for tests, inspections, or approvals where building codes or applicable laws or regulations require.

    A. Contractor
    B. Owner
    C. Architect
    D. Primary Qualifying Agent

Please See Answer Key on following page
ALH 02/15/2022

The following abbreviations are used in the Table below:

CM: Florida Contractors Manual

BGTA: Builders Guide to Accounting, 2001

A201, A401, A701: Various AIA documents

FBC: FL Building Code; Building/Residential/Existing Building/Energy Conservation/ Accessibility

Walker's: Walker's Building Estimator's Reference Book

OSHA: 29 CFR 1926 OSHA Construction Industry Regulations

PPCC: Principles and Practices of Commercial Construction

DCCM: Design and Control of Concrete Mixtures

Rebar: Placing Reinforcing Bars

Gypsum: Application and Finishing of Gypsum Panel Products, GA-216

EEBC: Energy Efficient Building Construction in Florida

Truss: BCSI Guide to Good Practice for handling, Installing, Restraining & Bracing of Metal Plate Connected Wood Trusses

TOC: Table of Contents

Question Answer Location (search hints in parentheses)

Question	Answer	Location (search hints in parentheses)
1	D	Sheet 2/15 and follow notes at top to sheet 10/15 Footing mark 3 – eight (8) footers 8' - 6" x 6' – 6" x 1' - 8" – convert to feet = 8.5 ft x 6.5 ft x 1.66 ft = 91.715 cft x 8 = 733.72 cft ÷ 27 cft/cyd = 27.17 cyd
2	D	Sheet 2/15 detail drawing A/2 – go to page 2
3	B	Sheet 11/15 - Inside dimension of each planter = 5.66 ft x 5.66 ft = 32.11 sqft 32.11 sqft x .83 ft= 26.65 cft per planter. 26.65 cft x 2 planters = 53.30 cft ÷ 27 cft/cyd = 1.97 cyd
4	C	Add up all sides – 456.0 ft + 254.0 ft + 457.9 ft + 141.4 ft + 20.0 ft + 156.0 ft = 1,485.3 ft minus 3 gates at 8 ft = 1,485.3 ft – 24 ft = 1,461.30 or 1,462 ft
5	D	Since you know that one leg of the 45° triangle is 50 yds, then the other leg is also 50 yds 75 yds + 50 yds + 50 yds = 175 yds
6	B	Calculate the perimeter of the property Line AC = $\sqrt{50^2 + 50^2}$ = $\sqrt{5000}$ = 70.71 yds – Pythagorean Theorem Line BD = line AC = 70.71 ~~yds~~ Line AB = 75 yds (given) Line CD = 175 yds (from previous question) Perimeter = AB + BD + AC + CD = 75 + 70.71 + 70.71 + 175 = 391.42 yds. 1 yd = 3 ft 391.42 yds x 3ft/yd = 1,174.26 feet 1,174.26 ft x $12/ft = $14,091.12
7	B	CM, pg. 10-38 (Index: "Project Administration")
8	B	FBC-Building, Sec: 110.3 (Index: "Inspections: Required")
9	A	Trade Knowledge - Margin of Profit = Net Income / Sales $120,000 - $90,000 = $30,000 $30,000 / $120,000 = .25 or 25%
10	B	CM, pg. 10-9 (Index: Bidding and TOC: Chap 10 "Plans and Specifications - Proposal")
11	B	FBC-Building, Sect 107.1 (TOC: "Submittal Documents")

12	B	CM, pgs. 4-8 thru 4-9 (Index: "Insurance – Business Liability" and TOC: Chap 4 "Business Liability Exposures")
13	B	FBC – Building, Sect 303.3 (Index: "Use and Occupancy")
14	B	FBC-Building, Sect 107.3.5 (Index: "Plan Review")
15	D	AIA A201, Sec: 3.11 (Index: "Documents and Samples at the Site")
16	A	CM, 2021 pgs. 2-19, 2-20; 2017 pgs. 2-7, 2-8 (Index: "Licensing – Subcontracting Requirements")
17	A	CM, 2021 pg. 9-80; 2017 pgs. 9-92, 9-93 §713.135(1)(d) (Index: "Notices: Notice of Commencement")
18	A	FBC-Building, Definitions
19	A	FBC-Building, Sec: 3202.2.3 (Index: "Awnings - Encroachment, public right-of-way")
20	C	FBC – Building, Sect [A] 107.5 ("Construction Documents – retainage")
21	A	CM, 2021 pg. 9-18; 2017 pg. 9-17 (Index: "Liens – Priority")
22	C	FBC-Building, 115.1 (Index: "Stop Work Order")
23	D	CM, 2021 pg. 7-36; 2017 pg. 7-37 (Index: "Osha – Safety Program")
24	D	FBC-Building, Sect 105.2 (Index: "Permits")
25	B	FBC-Building, 3109.1.2 (TOC: "Chapter 31 – Structures Seaward of a Coastal Construction Control Line")
26	B	CM, pg. 4-13 (Index: "Bonds – Surety")
27	D	CM, pg. 10-63 (Index: "Scheduling – Project Logic Table")
28	C	CM, pg. 4-17 (Index: "Financial Ratios")
29	C	CM, 2021 pgs. 2-30, 2-31, 2-84; 2017 pgs. 2-24, 2-95, 2-96 §489.129(1)(p) (Index: "Penalties – Licensing")
30	D	AIA A201, Sec: 11.5 2 (Index: "Insured Loss, Adjustment and Settlement of")
31	C	X (1.07) = $3,875 = $3,875 / 1.07 = $3,621.50 or $3,622
32	C	CM, pg. 10-7 (Index: "CSI Masterformat")
33	B	CM, 2021 pg. 2-76; 2017 pg. 2-86 §489.118 (Index: "Licensing, Grandfathering")
34	C	AIA A201, Sec: 3.7.4 (Index: "Concealed or unknown Conditions")
35	A	CM, pg. 3-74 (Index: "Loans – Types of "or "Discount Loans")
36	C	CM, 2021 pgs. 2-142; 2017 pg. 2-168 (Index: "Licensing - Demolition Specialty")
37	B	CM, 2021 pg. 2-6; 2017 pg. 2-6 (Index: "Licensing – Exemptions, Construction")
38	D	CM, 2021 pg. 9-41; 2017 pg. 9-41 (Index: "Liens - Fraudulent")
39	A	CM, 2021 pg. 9-36; 2017 pg. 9-36 (Index: "Liens – Sworn Statements")
40	B	CM, 2021 pg. 9-33; 2017 pg. 9-33 (Index: "Liens – Information Request")
41	B	AIA A201, Sec: 7.3.2 (Index: "Construction Change Directives")
42	A	CM, pg. 10-24 (TOC: Chap 10 "Estimates - Long Lead Items")
43	D	CM, pg. 10-97 (Index: "Environmental Compliance")
44	A	AIA A201, Sec: 7.3.1 (Index: "Construction Change Directives")
45	C	CM pg. 7-16 (Index: "OSHA – Retention")
46	D	AIA A201, Sec: 15.2.4 (Index: "Initial Decision Maker, Decisions")
47	C	CM, pg. 5-36 (Index: "Acts - Civil Rights – Florida")
48	A	CM, pg. 4-7 (Index: "Insurance – Property")
49	A	CM, 2021 pg. 7-32 (Index: "OSHA – Penalties")
	C	CM, 2017 pg. 7-32 (Index: "OSHA – Penalties")
50	A	3000ft x 10ft = 30,000 sqft 30,000 sqft – 20 windows (3ft x 4ft) or 240 sqft = 29,760 sqft 29,760 sqft x 2 coats = 59,520 total sqft 59,520 sqft / 200 sqft/hr = 297.6 hrs 297.6 hrs x $25/hr = $7,440

51	B	$266,000 x 45% (Estimated labor percentage) = $119,700 (Estimated labor cost) $119,700 x 85% = $101,745 (Actual labor cost)

		$119,700 - $101,745 = $17,955 additional profit
52	B	CM, 2021 pg. 10-60; 2017 pg. 10-60 (Index: "Scheduling – Activity List")
53	C	CM, 2021 pg. 1-14; 2017 pg. 1-15 (Index: "Fictitious Name")
54	C	CM, pg. 7-7 (Index: "Exemptions – OSHA and OSHA – Exempt Employers")
55	B	CM, pg. 5-45 (Index: "Acts – Public Whistle – blowers")
56	D	CM, 2021 pg. 2-22, 2-78; 2017 pg. 2-21, 2-89 §489.1195(2)(e) (Index: "Qualifying Agent")
57	B	AIA A201, Sec: 8.1.4 (Index: "Date of Substantial Completion")
58	D	CM, 2021 pg. 2-29; 2017 pg. 2-14 (Index: "Licensing – Unlicensed Activity")
59	C	AIA A201, Sec: 10.2.7 (Index: "Safety Precautions and Programs")
60	A	CM, 2021 pg. 2-28; 2017 pg. 2-12 (Index: "Employees – Types of Relationship")
61	B	FBC-Building, Sect 3105.3.1.4 (Index: "Awnings – Design and Construction")
62	D	CM, pg. 8-6 and 8-7 (Index: "Contracts – Written or Oral")
63	D	CM, pgs. 8-22 & 8-23 (Index: "Contracts - Defects")
64	D	388,000 lbs / 2,000 lbs/tons = 194 tons 194-ton x $65/ton = $12,610 (last year's rate) $12,610 x 1.07 = $13,492.70 (this year's delivery rate) $13,492.70 - $12,610 = $882.70 additional charge
65	B	AIA A201, Sec: 13.4.1 (Index: "Test and Inspections")

Contract Administration
Practice Exam #3

For Questions 1 through 4, refer to Plan Set #9501

1. The foundation footer marked with the following symbol appears _____ times on the foundation plan.

   A. 11
   B. 12
   C. 13
   D. 14

   ▽ 2

2. The installed height of the acoustical ceiling on the First Floor is _____ ft.

   A. 9
   B. 10
   C. 11
   D. 12

3. The interior walls and floor of the Elevator Pit are to be coated with a waterproofing compound. Each gallon covers 75 square feet of surface. The job requires three (3) coats. _____ gallons are required to be purchased. Round up to the nearest whole gallon.

   A. 9
   B. 3
   C. 6
   D. 10

4. The plans call for a total of _____ stair treads from the 2nd floor to the 4th floor.

   A. 22
   B. 44
   C. 66
   D. 88

Use the following site plan to answer questions 5 and 6.

The angle at point A= the angle at point B= the angle at point C= 90°.

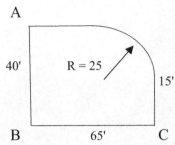

5. The diagonal distance from point A to point C is _____.

    A. 105'
    B. 76' 4"
    C. 145.5'
    D. 90'-10"

6. A landscape contractor has been hired to supply and install sod for this lot at the rate of $4.50 per square foot. The contract price is_____.

    A. Less than $10,000
    B. $10,000 to $10,499
    C. $10,500 to $10,999
    D. More than $11,000

7. A contractor is hired to dig an excavation in dry clay. Assume the percentage of swell is 35%. The bottom dimensions of the excavation are 200 ft. x 400 ft. The sides of the excavation are sloped at a rate of 1 to 1. The excavation is 10 feet deep. _____cubic yards of soil is to be excavated and removed from the site.

    A. Less than 35,000
    B. 42,000 to 44,999
    C. 45,000 to 49,999
    D. More than 50,000

8. _____requires a permit.

    A. The installation, replacement, removal or metering of any load management control device
    B. A portable cooling unit
    C. A self -contained refrigeration system containing 15 pounds of refrigerant and actuated by a 2 HP motor
    D. The installation of steam, hot or chilled water piping within any heating or cooling equipment regulated by the building code

9. The percentage of completion method will result in revenue recognition _____ the completed contract method.

    A. a little slower than
    B. about the same as
    C. more quickly than
    D. is the same as

10. A Change Order is prepared by _____.

    A. The Architect
    B. The Owner
    C. The Contractor
    D. The Initial Decision Maker

11. If an Owner breaches a Contract, or a Contractor breaches a Subcontract, by nonpayment of a non-material amount, _____.

    A. The contractor or subcontractor may terminate the contract after delivering a written notice and waiting for a period of 5 days.
    B. The contractor or subcontractor has 21 days to submit a claim to the Initial Dispute Resolver.
    C. The matter must be resolved through binding arbitration.
    D. There is no basis to terminate the Contract.

12. _____ contracts are normally negotiated between the owner and the contractor.

    A. Lump-sum
    B. Unit price
    C. Cost-plus
    D. Guaranteed maximum price

13. According to the AIA documents, "Contract Time" is the period of time allotted in the Contract Documents _____.

    A. For the Contractor to finish the Work
    B. From the Notice of Commencement to the Certificate of Occupancy
    C. For Substantial Completion of the Work
    D. From the signing of the Contract to the issuing of the Final Payment

14. A contractor is hired to apply three (3) coats of a waterproofing coating to the walls and floor of an equipment pit. The interior dimensions of the pit are 8'-4" x 8'-4". The depth of the pit is 6' -6". The coating only comes in one-gallon cans. Each gallon covers 30 square feet and a gallon costs $90. The contractor charges $1.12/SF to apply each coat. The total Material and Labor costs for this job is _____.

    A. $2,000 to $2,500
    B. $2,501 to $2,750
    C. $2,751 to $3,000
    D. $3,001 to $3,600

15. A _____ contract provides that a contractor will perform specific work and be paid per unit of output.

      A. Unit-price contract
      B. Time and material contract
      C. Lump-sum contract
      D. Guaranteed maximum price contract

16. The Contractor shall apply for progress payments _____.

      A. At least once a month for the duration of the Work
      B. At least ten days before the date established for each progress payment
      C. At intervals established by the Architect
      D. When the Work has reached a level of completion approved by the Architect

17. The _____ completes the Job Status Report for each project each month.

      A. Project Manager
      B. Field Superintendent
      C. Project Supervisor
      D. Field Supervisor

18. A permit is required for a temporary structure that is used for the gathering of _____ or more persons.

      A. 5
      B. 10
      C. 15
      D. 20

19. The _____ bond guarantees that a contractor, if awarded a bid, will enter into the contract at the stipulated price and supply the required performance and payment bonds.

      A. Supply
      B. Payment
      C. Contract
      D. Bid

20. The timing and sequence required for electrical inspections shall be _____.

      A. Underground, rough-in, final
      B. First, second, final
      C. Underground, intermediate, final
      D. Initial, rough-in, final

21. The FCRA Act applies to any employer which employs _____ or more employees for each working day in each of twenty or more calendar weeks in the current or preceding calendar year.

      A. 5
      B. 10
      C. 11
      D. 15

22. If framing lumber sells for $3.00/board foot, the cost of lumber required to build a 2 x 4 stud wall, 16" on center, 20' long x 10' high with single top and bottom plate is _____. Select the closest answer.

   A. $280.00
   B. $350.00
   C. $400.00
   D. $450.00

23. A Contractor submitted an application for a progress payment. The project has a $146,000 contract amount and was 46% complete at the time of the payment application. The Architect did not certify $22,000 of the requested amount. The retainage rate is 5%. The Contractor should expect to receive _____.

   A. $67,160
   B. $45,160
   C. $22,000
   D. $42,902

24. The total Labor and Material cost for a project was estimated to be $377,000 and 55% was estimated for Materials. The additional profit on the job if the actual Labor costs were only 85% of the estimated Labor costs will be _____.

   A. $16,965.00
   B. $25,447.50
   C. $14,402.50
   D. $31,102.50

25. The issuance of a Certificate for Payment by the Architect to the Owner constitutes a representation by the Architect that _____.

   A. The Work has progressed to the point indicated and is in accordance with the Contract Documents.
   B. The Architect has made exhaustive on-site inspections to check the quality and quantity of the Work.
   C. The Contractor has signed a partial waiver of lien for the amount requested.
   D. The Architect has reviewed and approved the Contractor's means, methods, techniques, sequences and procedures.

26. _____ does NOT require a construction contracting license.

   A. A contractor specializing in residential remodeling
   B. A contractor demolishing a water tower
   C. A local government employee
   D. A screen enclosure contractor

27. _____ does NOT require a building permit.

   A. Replacing a home's windows without altering the size of the openings
   B. Repairing a storm-damaged roof
   C. Reroofing an existing home without removing the existing shingles
   D. Installing a portable cooling unit

28. An addendum will be issued _____.

    A. At the discretion of the Architect
    B. No later than 4 days prior to the date for receipt of bids
    C. By the Architect in response to a written request from the Owner or Contractor for clarification of an item in the Bidding Documents
    D. By the Architect to the Contractor who has requested clarification of an item in the Bidding Documents

29. Reinforcing bars are designated by number. The number represents the approximate diameter of the bar in _____ inches.

    A. 1/8
    B. 1/4
    C. 1/6
    D. 1/2

30. Of the following terms, "offer, acceptance, description and consideration," _____ is NOT a term included in the customary definition of a contract.

    A. Offer
    B. Acceptance
    C. Description
    D. Consideration

31. A pedestrian walkway by a construction site shall have railings not less than _____ and be sufficient to direct pedestrians around construction areas.

    A. 8 feet in width
    B. 4 feet in width
    C. 42 inches in height
    D. 36 inches in height

32. Unless otherwise provided, performance and payment bonds shall be written on _____.

    A. AIA A312
    B. AIA A01
    C. AIA A201
    D. AIA E203

33. If an Owner occupies a portion of the project prior to completion, which of the following statements is true?

    A. Such partial occupancy constitutes the Owner's acceptance of that part of the Work only.
    B. The Owner's acceptance of that part of the work being partially occupied is contingent on the Architect's approval.
    C. The Owner's acceptance of that portion of the work is contingent on the Architect's certification of the Contractor's application for payment covering that portion of the work.
    D. Unless otherwise agreed upon, partial occupancy or use of a portion of the Work shall not constitute acceptance of Work not complying with the Contract Documents.

34. A contractor's license number does NOT have to appear _____.

    A. On business cards
    B. On free phone directory listings
    C. On billboards
    D. On flyers

35. The bidder shall deliver the required bonds to the Owner _____.

    A. Not later than three days following the date of execution of the Contract
    B. Upon demand but before the date of notice of commencement
    C. At the time and place specified in the Bidding Documents
    D. As a condition for the execution of the Contract

36. The U Factor for glazed block shall be _____.

    A. .35
    B. .50
    C. .60
    D. .80

37. Upon such assignment, if the Work has been suspended for more than _____ days, the Subcontractor's compensation shall be equitably adjusted for increases in cost resulting from the suspension.

    A. 14
    B. 28
    C. 30
    D. 45

38. If the amounts of payments misapplied has an aggregate value of $7,500, the violator is guilty of misapplication of construction funds and guilty of _____ .

    A. Felony
    B. Felony of first degree
    C. Felony of second degree
    D. Felony of third degree

39. A _____ contract benefits both the owner and contractor from value engineering that may be performed.

    A. Lump-sum
    B. Unit-price
    C. Cost-plus
    D. GMP (Guaranteed Maximum Price)

40. An applicant may become a certified construction contractor if he has at least _____ years' experience as a worker in that category at the time of application.

    A. 2
    B. 3
    C. 4
    D. 5

41. The _____ establishes the amount of liquidated damages that would result from a delay in completing the project.

    A. Owner
    B. Contractor
    C. Architect
    D. Surety

42. The Subcontractor shall notify the Contractor within _____ days of an injury to an employee or agent of the Subcontractor which occurred at the site.

    A. 3
    B. 5
    C. 7
    D. 10

43. Each agreement for repair, restoration, improvement, or construction to residential real property must contain a written statement explaining the consumer's rights under the recovery fund, except where the value of all labor and materials does not exceed _____ .

    A. $500
    B, $1,500
    C. $2,000
    D. $2,500

44. If an owner of an owner-occupied residential building obtains a permit to remove asbestos-containing material from that building, which of the following statements is NOT true.

    A. The owner, even though not licensed, may act as the asbestos abatement contractor.
    B. The owner may not sell or lease the property within 1 year after the asbestos abatement work is complete.
    C. The work must be done according to all local, state and federal laws and regulations which apply to asbestos abatement projects.
    D. None of the above. Under no circumstances is an owner of a residential building allowed to act as their own asbestos abatement contractor.

45. _____ owns the drawings, specifications and other instruments of service after the completion of project.

    A. Owner
    B. Architect
    C. Contractor
    D. None of the above

46. _____approves shop drawings from the structural steel fabricator.

    A. Owner
    B. Contractor
    C. Architect
    D. Initial Decision Maker

47. The Contractor shall permit the Subcontractor _____ information regarding the percentages of completion and the amount certified on account of Work done by the Subcontractor.

    A. To obtain from the Contractor
    B. To request directly from the Owner
    C. To obtain from the Surety
    D. To request directly from the Architect

48. A "Parking by Disabled Permit Only" sign shall be placed on or at least _____ feet above the finished floor or ground surface measured to the bottom of the sign.

    A. 4
    B. 4.5
    C. 5
    D. 5.5

49. _____ requires a permit.

    A. Chickees
    B. Tents and other temporary structures larger than 120 square feet
    C. Construction offices
    D. Temporary housing provided by the Dept of Corrections to prisoners in the state correctional system

50. Which of the following statements is NOT true regarding a building permit?

    A. A copy of the permit shall be kept on the site of the work until the completion of the project.
    B. Work shall be considered to be in active progress when the permit has received an approved inspection within 180 days.
    C. Work covered by the permit shall commence within 180 days after the permit issue date.
    D. With the building official's approval, work can begin prior to the issuing of the permit so long as the work does not proceed past the point of the first required inspection.

51. The penalty for a 1st violation of contracting without first obtaining a license in the State of Florida is a _____.

    A. First degree felony
    B. Third degree felony
    C. First degree misdemeanor
    D. Third degree misdemeanor

52. If a contractor incurs liquidated damages as a result of a default by a subcontractor, the contractor
_____.

        A. Will recover the cost of such damages from the subcontractor
        B. Will recover the cost of such damages from the subcontractor's liability insurance provider
        C. Will not be able to recover the cost of the liquidated damages from the subcontractor unless there is
        a specific clause in the subcontract allowing for a pass-through
        D. Can submit his claim for the amount of such damages to the Initial Dispute Resolver

53. In cases of Claims for additional time due to a continuing delay, _____.

        A. The Contractor must resubmit his Claim weekly for each week the delay continues.
        B. The allowance for additional time is capped at four weeks.
        C. Only one Claim is necessary.
        D. The Claim must be mediated before going to binding arbitration.

54. Repairs to an existing building located seaward of a coastal construction control line _____.

        A. Shall not exceed 20 percent of the replacement value of the existing building
        B. Shall be designed to resist the predicted forces of a 100-year storm surge, storm waves or other
        predictable weather conditions
        C. Shall be designed by a registered design professional
        D. All of the above

55. Carpet or carpet tile pile height shall be _____ inch maximum.

        A. 1/4
        B. 1/2
        C. 3/4
        D. 7/8

56. The _____ conducts the safety meetings and prepares the minutes.

        A. Project Manager
        B. Project Superintendent
        C. Safety Director
        D. Field Supervisor

57. If the lienor fails to file a lawsuit to enforce the lien within ____ days of the date the clerk of court certifies
in the Notice of Contest of Lien that a copy was served on the lienor, lien rights are lost.

        A. 30
        B. 45
        C. 60
        D. 90

58. Trusses are inspected _____.

        A. By the building official during the framing inspection
        B. By the building official during the roofing inspection
        C. By the building official during the sheathing inspection
        D. By the building official during the final inspection

59. A Subcontractor shall furnish to the Contractor periodic progress reports on the Work of the Subcontract _____.

    A. Weekly
    B. Bi-weekly
    C. At mutually agreed upon intervals
    D. At the time of each application for Progress Payment

60. Construction materials and equipment shall not be placed or stored within _____ feet of a street intersection.

    A. 5
    B. 10
    C. 15
    D. 20

61. A contractor places the following order for several types of structural steel.
    • 24 pieces W12x45 x 16 feet
    • 18 pieces S24x100 x 12 feet
    • 18 pieces C12x20.7 x 20 feet

If structural steel sells for $1,000 per ton, the contractor will expect to pay _____ for this order. Select the closest answer.

    A. $46,500
    B. $23,200
    C. $69,500
    D. $100,000

62. When a lien amount is less than _____, it may be enforced or foreclosed in the county court.

    A. $2,500
    B. $5,000
    C. $10,000
    D. $15,000

63. Unless otherwise provided in the Contract Documents, _____ shall secure and pay for the building permit.

    A. The Owner
    B. The Contractor
    C. Either the Owner or the Contractor
    D. The Architect

64. The difference in the minimum penalty fines between a first offense and a repeat offense for contracting with a delinquent license is _____.

    A. $500
    B. $750
    C. $1,000
    D. $1,500

65. A ramp has a rise of 7 ½" over a distance of 200 feet, the slope or grade will be _____.

    A. .001 or 1%
    B. .002 or .2%
    C. .003 or .3%
    D. .0375 or 3.75%

Please See Answer Key on following page
ALH 2/16/22

127

1 Exam Prep
Contract Administration
Practice Exam #3 Answers

The following abbreviations are used in the Table below:

CM: Florida Contractors Manual
BGTA: Builders Guide to Accounting, 2001
A201, A401, A701: Various AIA documents
FBC: FL Building Code; Building/Residential/Existing Building/Energy Conservation/ Accessibility
Walker's: Walker's Building Estimator's Reference Book
OSHA: 29 CFR 1926 OSHA Construction Industry Regulations
PPCC: Principles and Practices of Commercial Construction
DCCM: Design and Control of Concrete Mixtures
Rebar: Placing Reinforcing Bars
Gypsum: Application and Finishing of Gypsum Panel Products, GA-216
EEBC: Energy Efficient Building Construction in Florida
Truss: BCSI Guide to Good Practice for handling, Installing, Restraining & Bracing of Metal Plate Connected Wood Trusses
TOC: Table of Contents

Question Answer Location (search hints in parentheses)

1	D	Sheet 2/15, "Foundation Plan."
2	C	Sheet 4/15, Detail Drawing ¼
3	A	Sheet 2/15, Walls: interior perimeter = (8.33ft + 9.33ft+ 8.33ft+ 9.33ft= 35.33ft Interior wall height = 4 ft Walls: 35.33ft x 4ft = 141.28 sqft Floor: 8.33ft x 9.33ft = 77.72 sqft for the floor 141.28 sqft + 77.72 sqft = 219 sqft x 3 coats= 657 sqft 657 sqft / 75 sqft /gal = 8. 76 gallons or 9 full gallons.
4	D	Sheet 10/15, Detail Drawing 1/10 shows that each run of stairs has 12 Risers. Risers (12) – 1 = 11 treads. In each stairwell, there are 4 runs of stairs from the 2nd floor landing to the 4th floor landing Sheet 3/15 shows two (2) stairwells in the building Total treads = 11 x 4 x 2 = 88
5	B	Right triangle – Pythagorean Theorem – $(Line\ AB)^2 + (Line\ BC)^2 = (Line\ AC)^2$ so Line AC is equal to the square root of $\sqrt{40^2 + 65^2} = \sqrt{1600 + 4225} = 76.32$ ft or 76' – 4"
6	D	Divide up into known shapes which are rectangles one is 40ft x 40ft = 1,600sqft and one is 25ft x 15ft = 375sqft and one ¼ circle with radius 25ft = πr^2 /4 = (π x 25^2) / 4 = 1,963.49 sqft / 4 = 490.87sqft. Total square footage = 1,600sqft + 375sqft + 490.87sqft = 2,465.87sqft Contract cost= 2,465.87 sqft x \$4.50/sqft = \$11,096.42
7	B	Trade Knowledge – PPCC – 9th edition page 72 and 10th edition page 77

Depth of excavation = 10 ft sides are sloped at 1 to 1

Each side sloped back 10 feet so add 10 ft to each side

Average area method to calculate

$$\frac{\text{Bottom Area} + \text{Top Area}}{2} \times 10 \text{ feet} = \text{Volume of excavation}$$

Bottom Area = 200 ft x 400 ft = 80,000 sqft

Top Area = [(200ft + 10 ft + 10ft) x (400ft + 10 ft + 10 ft)]

          220 ft x 420 ft = 92,400sqft

Volume = (80,000sqft + 92,400sqft) = 172,400 sqft / 2 = 86,200 sqft x 10ft = 862,000 cft and 862,000 cft ÷ 27 cft /cyd = 31,925.92 cyd

Swell factor for Dry Clay is 35%.

31,925.92 cyd x 1.35 = 43,100 cyd to be hauled away

8	C	FBC-Building, sect 105.2 (Index: "Permits")
9	C	CM, pg. 3-79 (Index: "Percentage of Completion")
10	A	AIA A201, art. 7.2.1. (Index: "Change Orders, Definition of.")
11	D	CM, pg. 8-24 (Index: "Contracts – Breach")
12	C	CM, pg. 10-34 (Index: "Type of Contracts")
13	C	AIA A201, art. 8.1.1. (Index: "Contract and Time, Definition of")
14	D	The interior dimension of the pit is 8.33' x 8.33' The depth of the pit = 6.5 ft Square footage for the four (4) walls = walk around like a painter with a wheel 8.33ft + 8.33ft + 8.33ft + 8.33ft = 33.32 ft x 6.5 ft = 216.58 sqft Square footage of the pit floor = 8.33ft x 8.33ft = 69.39 sqft Total square footage = (216.58 sqft + 69.39 sqft) = 285.97 x 3 coats = 857.91 sqft Labor cost = 857. 91 sqft x $1.12/sqft = $960.85 Material cost = 857.91 sqft ÷ 30 sqft/gal = 28.59 gal or 29-gal x $90 = $2,610 Total Labor and Material = $960.85 + $2,610 = $3,570.85
15	A	CM, pg. 3-79 (Index: "Type of Contracts")
16	B	AIA A201, art. 9.3.1. (Index: "Progress Payments")
17	B	CM, pg. 10-38 (Index: "Project Administration" and TOC: Chap 10 "Sample Job Cost Records – Project Administration")
18	B	FBC-Building, sect 3103.1.2 (Temporary Structures - Permit)
19	D	CM, pg. 4-13 (Index: "Bonds – Types of Bonds") and TOC: Chap 4 "Suretyship - Types of Bonds")
20	A	FBC-Building, sect 110.3 (Index: "Inspections-Required")
21	D	CM, pg. 5-35 (Index: "Acts – Civil Rights - Florida")
22	C	Trade Knowledge – board feet Walker's, (32nd Ed.) Pgs. 376, 379 (31st Ed.) Pgs. 633, 636 20 ft long/ 16"/12" on center = 15 studs + 1 extra on end @ 10 ft high = 160 ft Top plate is 20 ft and Bottom plate is 20 ft = 40 ft – add all the lineal footage together = 160 ft + 20 ft + 20 ft = 200 ft 2 x 4 x 200 ft / 12 = 133.33 board feet x $3.00/board ft = $400.00

23	D	$146,000 x 46% = $67,160 The Architect did not certify $22,000 $67,160 - $22,000 = $45,160 The retainage rate is 5%. $45,160 - 5% ($45,160) = $42,902 or $45,160 x 95% = $42,902
24	B	$377,000 x 45% = $169,650 (original ESTIMATED Labor cost). $169,650 x 85% = $144,202.50 (ACTUAL Labor cost). $169,650 - $144,202.50 = $25,447.50 additional profit.
25	A	AIA, A201, art. 9.4.2 (Index: "Certificates for Payment")
26	C	CM, 2021 pgs. 2-18, 2-19; 2017 pgs. 2-6, 2-7 (Index: "Licensing – Exemptions, Construction" and TOC: Chap 2 "State Contractor Certification -Licensing Exemptions - Construction Contracting")
27	D	FBC-Building, sect 105.2 (Index: "Permits")
28	B	AIA A701, art. 3.4.3. (TOC: Chapter 3 - Bidding Documents)
29	A	Trade Knowledge - #5 bar is 5 x 1/8 = 5/8" or .625 "in diameter Rebar – 9th edition 6-1/6-2 and 10th edition 7-1/7-2
30	C	CM, pg. 8-5. (Index: "Contracts – Defined" and TOC: Chap. 8 "What is a contract?")
31	C	FBC-Building, sect 3306.4 (Index: "Pedestrian, Protection at construction site")
32	A	AIA A701, art. 7.2.2 (TOC Chapter 7: "Performance Bond and Payment Bond")
33	D	AIA A201, art. 9.9.3 (Index: "Partial Occupancy or Use")
34	B	CM, 2021 pg. 2-124; 2017 pg. 2-149 §61G4-12.011(3) Need TAB for all advertisement requirements
35	A	AIA A701, art. 7.2.1 (Article 7: "Performance Bond and Payment Bond")
36	C	FBC-Energy Conservation, Table R303.1.3(1) (Index: "Window Area – See Fenestration and Glazing Area – Rating and labeling")
37	C	AIA A201, art. 5.4.2. (Index: "Subcontractual Relations")
38	C	CM, 2021 pg. 9-93; 2017 pg. 9-120 §713.345(1)(b)(2) (Index: "Moneys Received by Contractor" and TOC:" Misapplication of Funds")
39	D	CM, pgs. 10-35 (Index: "Type of Contracts")
40	C	CM, 2021 pgs. 2-6, 2-7; 2017 pg. 2-15 (Index: "Licensing – Certified Contractor")
41	A	CM, pg. 8-13 (Index: "Contracts – Liquidated Damages" and TOC: Chap 8 "Contract Terms - Liquidated Damages")
42	A	AIA A401, art. 4.4.1 (TOC: Chapter 4 - Subcontractor)
43	D	CM, 2021 pgs. 2-105; 2017 pg. 2-105 (Index: "Homeowners Recovery Fund – Duty to Notify")
44	D	FBC-Building, section 105.3.6 (Index: "Permits" and TOC: Chap 1 "Scope and Administration – Permits")
45	B	AIA A201, art. 1.5.1 (Index: "Ownership and Use of Drawings . . .")
46	C	AIA A201, art. 3.12.7 (Index: "Shop Drawings, Product Data and Samples."
47	D	AIA A401, art. 3.3.3 (TOC: Chapter 3 - Contractor)
48	C	FBC – Accessibility, sect 502.6.1 (TOC: "Chapter 5: General Site and Building Elements – Parking Spaces.")
49	B	FBC-Building, sect 3103.1.2 (Index: "Temporary Structures - Permit")
50	C	FBC-Building, sect 105.4 thru 105.12 (Index: "Permits")
51	C	CM, 2021 pg. 2-29; 2017 pg. 2-14 (Index: "Licensing - Penalties for Unlicensed Activity")

52	C	CM, pg. 8-14. (TOC, Chap 8: "Liquidated Damages" and Index: Contracts – Liquidated Damages)
53	C	AIA A201, art. 15.1.6.1 (Index: "Claims for Additional Time.")
54	B	FBC-Building, sect 3109.1 (TOC: Chap 31 "Special Construction- Structures Seaward of a Coastal Construction Control Line")
55	B	FBC – Accessibility, sect 302.2 (TOC: "Chapter 3: Building Blocks: Floor or Ground Surfaces.")
56	B	CM, 2021 pg. 2-29; 2017 pg. 10-72. (Index: "Job Responsibilities")
57	C	FBC-Residential R202 (Index: "Basement and Story")
58	A	FBC-Building, sect. 110.3 (Index: "Inspections, Required")
59	C	CM, 2021 pg. 9-31; 2017 pg. 9-31. (Index: "Lien - Duration")
60	D	FBC-Building, sect. 3308.1.1 (Index: "Safeguards During Construction – Temporary use of streets, alleys and public property")
61	B	Trade Knowledge – Size of standard steel shapes indicates depth and weight W12 x 45 – 12" deep and weighs 45 lbs. per foot S24 x 100 – 24" deep and weighs 100 lbs. per foot C12 x 20.7 – 12" deep and weighs 20.7 lbs. per foot 16 ft x 45 lb/ft = 720 lbs x 24 pieces = 17,280 lbs. 12 ft x 100 lb/ft = 1,200 lbs x 18 pieces = 21,600 lbs. 20 ft x 20.7 lb/ft = 414 lbs x 18 pieces = 7,452 lbs. Total weight = 46,332 lbs. / 2000 lbs./ton = 23.166 tons 23.166 tons x \$1000/ton = \$23,166
62	D	CM, 2021 pg. 9-46; 2017 pg. 9-46. (Index: "Lien - Releases")
63	B	AIA A201, art. 3.7.1. (Index: "Building Permit.")
64	C	CM, 2021 pg. 2-185; 2017 pg. 2-185. Insert TAB – Disciplinary Summary
65	C	Trade Knowledge – Walker's (32nd Ed.) Pgs. 762 – 763 (31st Ed.) Pg. 1244 Convert inches to feet – 7 ½ / 12 inches in a foot = 0.63 ft Rise over run = slope x 100% = grade 0.63 feet / 200 feet = .003 slope or x 100% = .3% grade

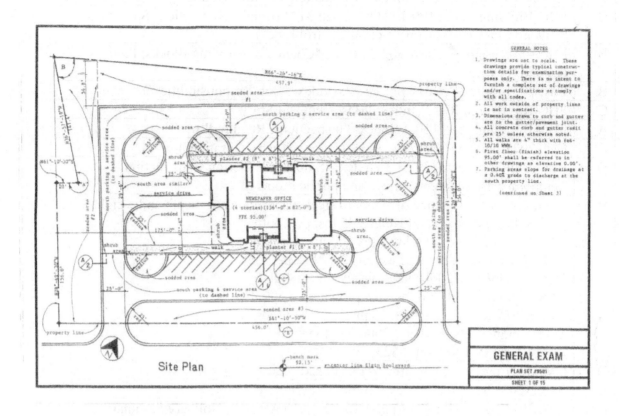

Site Plan

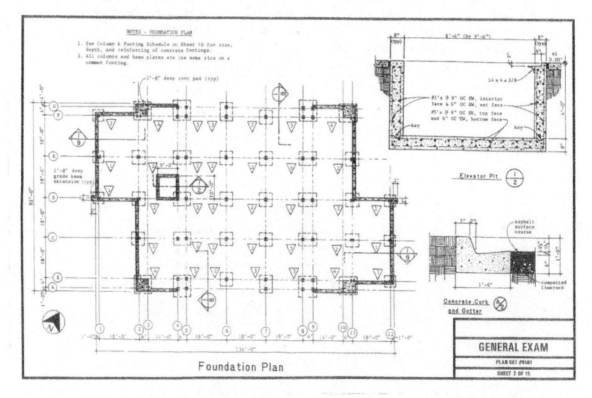

Elevator Pit 1/2

Concrete Curb and Gutter A/2

Foundation Plan

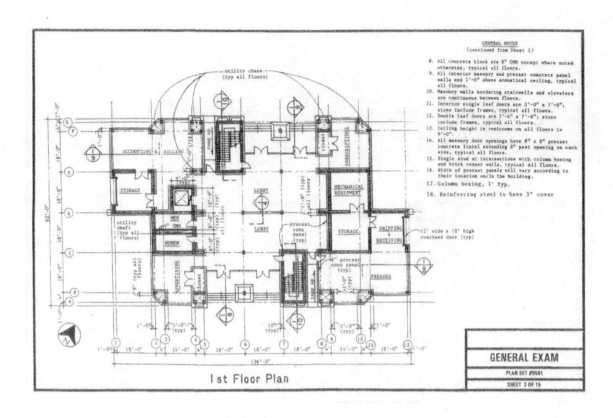

8. All concrete block are 8" CMU except where noted otherwise, typical all floors.
9. All interior masonry and precast concrete panel walls end 1'-0" above acoustical ceiling, typical all floors.
10. Masonry walls bordering stairwells and elevators are continuous between floors.
11. Interior single leaf doors are 3'-0" x 7'-0"; sizes include frames, typical all floors.
12. Double leaf doors are 5'-6" x 7'-0"; sizes include frames, typical all floors.
13. Ceiling height in restrooms on all floors is 9'-0".
14. All masonry door openings have 8" x 8" precast concrete lintel extending 8" past opening on each side, typical all floors.
15. Single stud at intersections with column boxing and brick veneer walls, typical all floors.
16. Width of precast panels will vary according to their location on/in the building.
17. Column boxing, 1' Typ.
18. Reinforcing steel to have 3" cover

1st Floor Plan

GENERAL EXAM
PLAN SET #9501
SHEET 3 OF 15

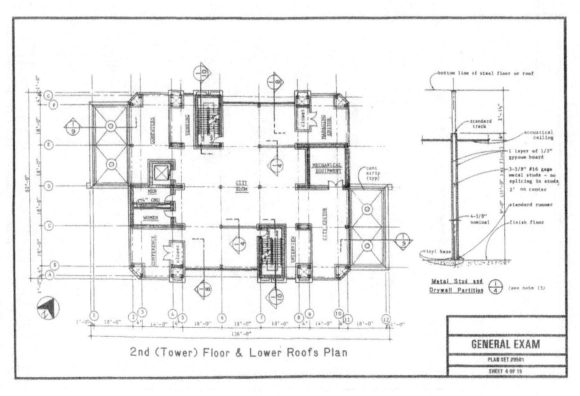

2nd (Tower) Floor & Lower Roofs Plan

Metal Stud and
Drywall Partition (see note 15)

GENERAL EXAM
PLAN SET #9501
SHEET 4 OF 15

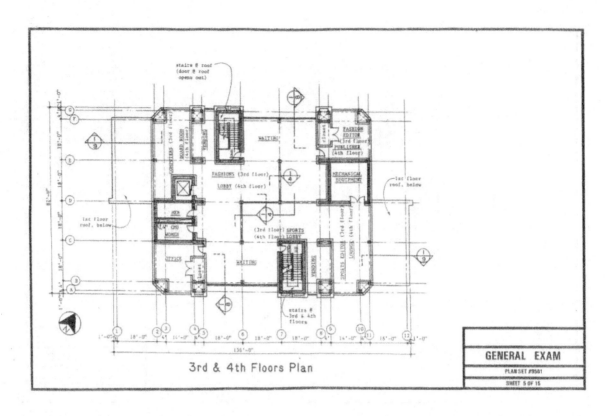

3rd & 4th Floors Plan

GENERAL EXAM

PLAN SET #9501

SHEET 5 OF 15

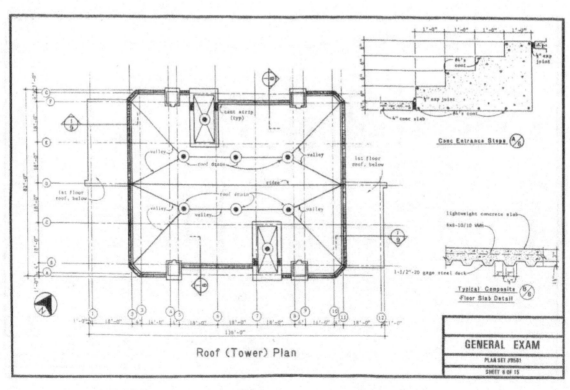

Roof (Tower) Plan

Conc Entrance Steps

Typical Composite
Floor Slab Detail

GENERAL EXAM

PLAN SET #9501

SHEET 6 OF 15

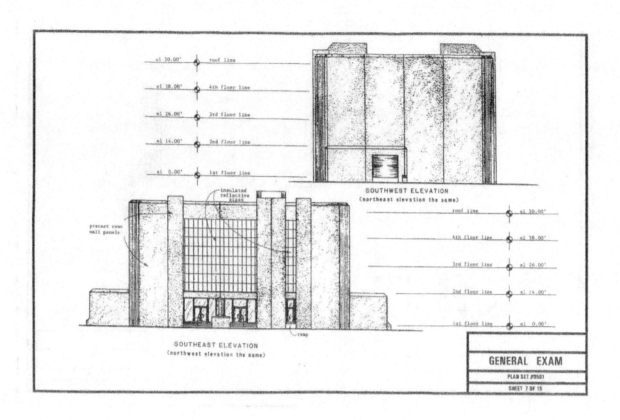

el 50.00'   roof line

el 38.00'   4th floor line

el 26.00'   3rd floor line

el 14.00'   2nd floor line

el 0.00'   1st floor line

SOUTHWEST ELEVATION
(northeast elevation the same)

insulated reflective glass

precast conc wall panels

roof line   el 50.00'

4th floor line   el 38.00'

3rd floor line   el 26.00'

2nd floor line   el 14.00'

1st floor line   el 0.00'

ramp

SOUTHEAST ELEVATION
(northwest elevation the same)

GENERAL EXAM

PLAN SET #9501

SHEET 7 OF 15

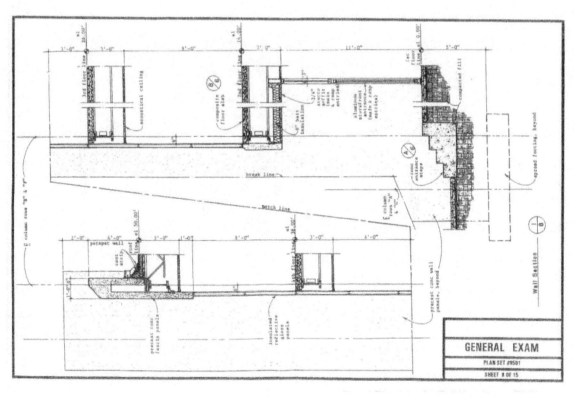

GENERAL EXAM

PLAN SET #9501

SHEET 8 OF 15

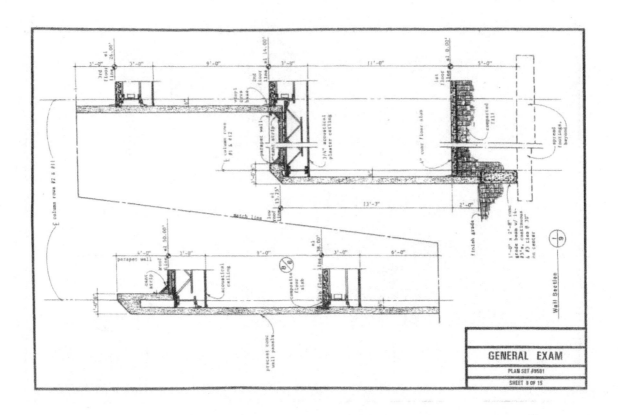

Wall Section

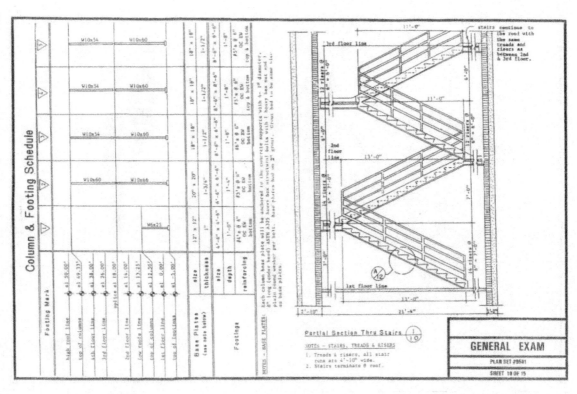

Column & Footing Schedule

Partial Section Thru Stairs

NOTES - STAIRS, TREADS & RISERS

1. Treads & risers, all stair runs are 4'-10" wide.
2. Stairs terminate @ roof.

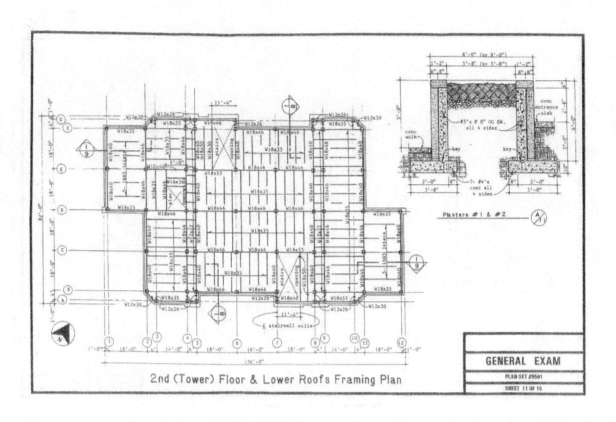

Planters #1 & #2   A/1

2nd (Tower) Floor & Lower Roofs Framing Plan

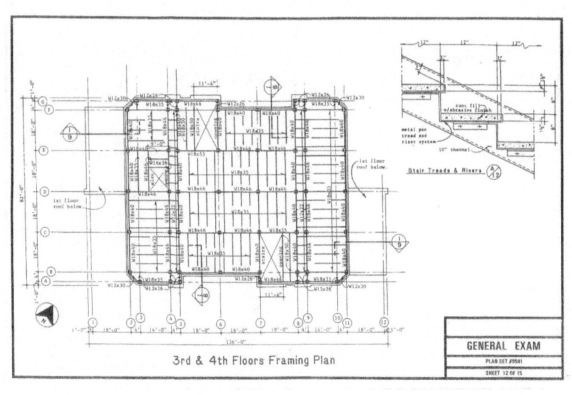

Stair Treads & Risers   A/12

3rd & 4th Floors Framing Plan

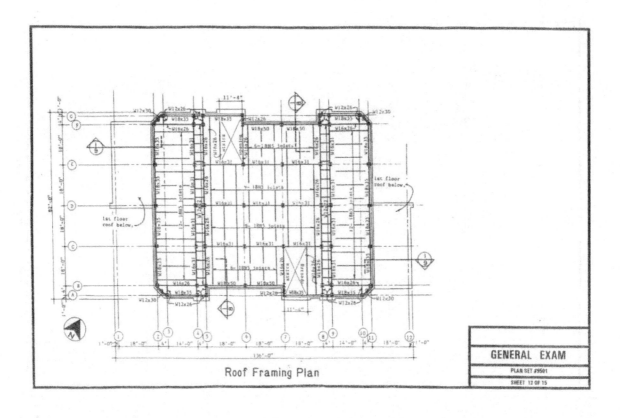

Roof Framing Plan

Symbol Legend

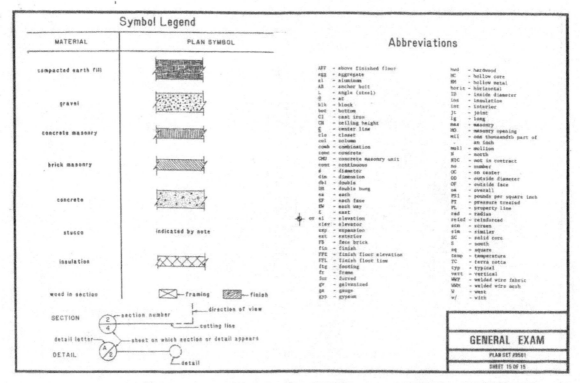

MATERIAL	PLAN SYMBOL
compacted earth fill	
gravel	
concrete masonry	
brick masonry	
concrete	
stucco	indicated by note
insulation	
wood in section	framing, finish

SECTION — section number, direction of view, cutting line

DETAIL — detail letter, sheet on which section or detail appears, detail

Abbreviations

AFF — above finished floor
agg — aggregate
al — aluminum
AB — anchor bolt
L — angle (steel)
@ — at
blk — block
bot — bottom
CI — cast iron
CH — ceiling height
₵ — center line
clo — closet
col — column
comb — combination
conc — concrete
CMU — concrete masonry unit
cont — continuous
∅ — diameter
dim — dimension
dbl — double
DH — double hung
ea — each
EF — each face
EW — each way
E — east
el — elevation
elev — elevator
exp — expansion
ext — exterior
FB — face brick
fin — finish
FFE — finish floor elevation
FFL — finish floor line
ftg — footing
fr — frame
fur — furred
gv — galvanized
ga — gauge
GYP — gypsum

hwd — hardwood
HC — hollow core
HM — hollow metal
horiz — horizontal
ID — inside diameter
ins — insulation
int — interior
jt — joint
lg — long
mas — masonry
MO — masonry opening
mil — one thousandth part of an inch
mull — mullion
N — north
NIC — not in contract
no — number
OC — on center
OD — outside diameter
OF — outside face
oa — overall
PSI — pounds per square inch
PT — pressure treated
PL — property line
rad — radius
reinf — reinforced
scn — screen
sim — similar
SC — solid core
S — south
sq — square
temp — temperature
TC — terra cotta
typ — typical
vert — vertical
WWF — welded wire fabric
WWM — welded wire mesh
W — west
w/ — with

Contract Administration
Practice Test #4

1. The filter lens shade number to be used when light cutting up to 1 inch shall be _____.

    A.   2
    B.   3 or 4
    C.   4 or 5
    D.   5 or 6

2. If an infringement of a copyright or patent is discovered by, or made known to, the Contractor, the _____ shall be responsible for the loss unless the information is promptly furnished to the Architect.

    A.   Engineer
    B.   Architect
    C.   Owner
    D.   Contractor

3. A contractor is performing an estimate on a building with drawings scaled to 3/8" = 1' 0". The contractor then measures 4 (7/8)" on the drawings as _____

    A.   8' 6"
    B.   12' 0"
    C.   13' 0"
    D.   14' 6"

4. The contractor's final payment affidavit must be delivered to the owner no later than _____ days before suit is filed to enforce the contractor's lien, even if the final payment has not yet become due.

    A.   5
    B.   10
    C.   15
    D.   30

5. Those liens to be paid last are the _____.

    A.   Liens of all persons other than laborers, payable in full of pro rata according to the amounts of their claims.
    B.   Liens of the architect/engineer
    C.   Liens of the contractor
    D.   Liens of all laborers

6. It is important that slab formwork measuring 42'-0" x 74'-0" be square before concrete is poured. The diagonal measurement to ensure the formwork would be square is_____. Select the closest answer.

   A.   85'-1"
   B.   85'-2"
   C.   85'-8"
   D.   85'-10"

7. The thickness of blown-in insulation shall be written in inches on markers that are installed at least one for every _____ square feet throughout the attic space.

   A.   50
   B.   100
   C.   200
   D.   300

8. Where equipment replacements and repairs must be performed in an emergency situation, the permit application shall be _____ .

   A.   Submitted 24 hours after the replacement/repair has been completed
   B.   Submitted the next business day after the replacement/repair has been completed
   C.   Submitted the next working business day after the replacement/repair has been completed
   D.   Submitted 24 hours after the replacement/repair has been started

9. A secondary qualifying agent has pulled a permit for a building project. There is a problem with payment to a subcontractor, the _____is (are) responsible for the payment to the subcontractor.

   A.   Primary qualifying agent
   B.   Secondary qualifying agent
   C.   Primary and secondary qualifying agents
   D.   Owner

10. The Workers' Compensation Law Act requires the employers carry insurance to cover employee's economic losses resulting from on-the-job injuries, regardless of fault, and the penalty for not carrying this insurance is a fine of not more than _____ and a possible criminal conviction.

   A. $250
   B. $500
   C. $750
   D. $1,000

11. Asbestos can only be removed by a _____.

   A.   FDEP Contractor
   B.   Licensed Asbestos Contractor
   C.   Licensed Asbestos Consultant
   D.   Licensed Demolition Contractor

12. The Subcontractor shall make all Claims promptly to the Contractor for additional cost, extensions of time and damages for delays and such claims shall be received by the Contractor not less than _____ days preceding the time by which the Contractor's Claim under the Prime Contract must be made.

    A.   Two working days
    B.   Two calendar days
    C.   Five working days
    D.   Five calendar days

13. If a contractor receives a deposit of $20,000 on a contract requiring a building permit with a total contract value of $150,000, he must apply for the applicable building permit within _____ days.

    A.   45
    B.   90
    C.   30
    D.   60

4. A claim of lien is effective for _____ from the date on which it is recorded.

    A.   45 days
    B.   60 days
    C.   1 year
    D.   90 days

5. The Owner shall furnish to the Contractor, within _____ days after receipt of written request, information necessary for the Contractor to evaluate, give notice of, or enforce mechanic's lien rights.

    A.   5
    B.   7
    C.   10
    D.   15

6. Orders imposing disciplinary action for local disciplinary action against a contractor shall contain all of the following except _____.

    A.   Clear statement of violations being charged
    B.   A recommendation to the CILB for actions to be taken
    C.   Findings of the facts
    D.   An invoice for all fines and penalties

7. Addenda will be issued no later than _____ days prior to the date for receipt of Bids.

    A.   3
    B.   4
    C.   7
    D.   10

18. The owner may terminate the period of effectiveness of a notice of commencement by recording a notice of termination that contains a statement of the date as of which the notice of commencement is terminated, which date may not be earlier than _____ days after the notice of termination is recorded.

    A.   15
    B.   20
    C.   30
    D.   45

19. A _____ provides a monthly indication of the contract value, cost expenses to date as well as a projection of costs to complete each item of work.

    A.   Monthly labor distribution report
    B.   Cost report summary
    C.   Monthly labor distribution analysis
    D.   Monthly indicated outcome report

20. The contractor shall promptly provide notice to the owner and architect before conditions are disturbed and in no event later than _____ days after first observance of the conditions.

    A.   7
    B.   21
    C.   3
    D.   14

21. Billings for work performed or costs incurred by one party that, in accordance with the agreement, should have been performed or incurred by the party to whom billed is called _____.

    A.   Change orders
    B.   Back charges
    C.   Incidental expenses
    D.   Billable expenses

22. The project construction schedule should be updated at least once every _____ days.

    A.   3
    B.   7
    C.   20
    D.   30

23. The number of squares of roofing materials to be ordered for a roof with dimensions 68' x 62' 6" and a pitch of 5/12 is _____. Select the closest answer.

    A.   42.50
    B.   46.50
    C.   51.50
    D.   55.50

24. Prior to the settlement of an insured loss, Owner shall notify Contractor the terms of the proposed settlement and the Contractor shall have _____ days from receipt of notice to object to the proposed settlement or allocation of the proceeds.

    A.   7
    B.   10
    C.   14
    D.   15

25. The _____ owns the float.

    A.   Owner
    B.   Contractor
    C.   First to use
    D.   Last to use

26. The Contractor has achieved substantial completion on a $1,380,200 contract. Previously payments made total $987,300 and a 10% retainage was being held. The current payment due is _____.

    A. $266,606
    B. $267,213
    C. $266,393
    D. $254,880

27. The maximum fine to be imposed for obtaining a license through fraud or misrepresentation is _____.

    A. $2,500
    B. $5,000
    C. $7,500
    D. $10,000

28. The issuance of a Certificate for Payment will constitute a representation by the _____ that the work has progressed to the point indicated and the quality of work is in accordance with the Contract Documents.

    A.   Contractor
    B.   Subcontractor
    C.   Architect
    D.   Owner

29. The slope of a parking lot that drops 8" in 90 is _____.

    A.   .088
    B.   .0063
    C.   .0074
    D.   .0088

30. The Notice of Commencement shall be the responsibility of _____ to be recorded in the Clerk's office prior to commencing work.

    A.   The Contractor
    B.   The Owner
    C.   The Authorized agent
    D.   Anyone

31. A permit issued shall be come invalid if the work authorized by such permit is suspended or abandoned for a period of _____ after the time the work is commenced.

    A.   30 days
    B.   60 days
    C.   180 days
    D.   6 months

32. The grade of a parking lot that drops 8" in 90 is _____%.

    A.   .63
    B.   .74
    C.   .88
    D.   8.88

33. Under the completed contract method, the contractor may recognize the profit _____.

    A.   When the final payment is accepted by the Owner
    B.   When the contract is 50% complete
    C.   When the project is nearly complete
    D.   When the architect signs off on the final release

34. If there is a 47 ft long 2 x 4 x 8 ft partition wall with the studs spaced 16" on center and it has a double top plate and a single base plate, _____ bd ft will be ordered to build this wall.

    A.   197.33
    B.   259.99
    C.   291.33
    D.   322.66

35. The subcontractor shall correct, repair or replace defective work within _____ hours after receiving notice of defective work from contractor.

    A.   24
    B.   36
    C.   48
    D.   60

36. A HP 14 x 89 weighs _____ lbs. per square foot.

    A. 14
    B. 28
    C. 75
    D. 89

37. The _____ method for recording income is the most preferred method for accounting statement presentation.

    A. Completed contract
    B. Percentage of completion
    C. Accrual-based accounting
    D. Cash-based accounting

38. For a labor (manpower) estimate, there are various factors which affect production and would include all of the following except_____,

    A. Size of crew
    B. Skill & experience of craft workers
    C. Supervision available on site
    D. Site accessibility

39. A room or space used for assembly purposes less than 750 square feet in area and accessory to another occupancy shall be classified as an _____ occupancy.

    A. Group A-1
    B. Group A-2
    C. Group B
    D. Group B-1

40. _____ means that goods first added to inventory are assumed to be the first goods sold from inventory.

    A. Item by item
    B. FIFO
    C. LIFO
    D. Average cost

41. A good preliminary labor estimate should vary less than _____ percent.

    A. 2.5
    B. 5
    C. 10
    D. 15

42. The CSI MasterFormat classification system has _____ technical divisions.

    A.   48
    B.   49
    C.   50
    D.   51

43. Claims by either the Owner or Contractor shall be initiated within _____ days after occurrence of the event giving rise to such claim or within _____ days after the claimant first recognizes the condition, whichever is later.

    A.   7
    B.   14
    C.   21
    D.   30

44. The business organization must notify DBPR of the termination of the qualifying agent and obtain another qualifying agent with _____ days.

    A.   30
    B.   45
    C.   60
    D.   90

45. The Contractor shall pay the Subcontractor each progress payment no later than _____ working days after the Contractor receives payment from the Owner.

    A.   5
    B.   7
    C.   10
    D.   14

46. After relocating his business to a new location, the Contractor has _____ days to notify the Board office of his new address.

    A.   10
    B.   21
    C.   30
    D.   45

47. An order for a minor change in the Work may be issued by the _____ alone.

    A.   Contractor
    B.   Owner
    C.   Architect
    D.   Subcontractor

48. Laborers that are average trained, have fair morale and a normal absence rate would have a production efficiency rate of _____ percent.

    A.   10 to 35
    B.   25 to 45
    C.   55 to 85
    D.   85 to 95

49. If a restaurant has an approved occupancy for 1,000 people, the minimum number of required accessible parking spaces shall be _____.

    A.   10
    B.   15
    C.   20
    D.   25

50. The Architect will have control over or charge of all the following except for _____.

    A.   Subcontractors
    B.   Contractor submitted shop drawings
    C.   Contractor submitted product data
    D.   Submitted samples

51. In the event of the death of the qualifying agent, _____ may finish an existing project that is under contract with the deceased qualifier.

    A.   Any one
    B.   A secondary qualifier
    C.   The spouse of the contractor
    D.   The owner

52. Elevators shall be provided with Phase I emergency recall operation and Phase II emergency in-car operation in accordance with _____.

    A.   ASME A16.1
    B.   ASME A17.1
    C.   CSA B42
    D.   CSA B43

53. _____ insurance covers subcontractor materials on job sites, while in transit or while stored at temporary locations.

    A.   Installation floater
    B.   Builders risk
    C.   Umbrella
    D.   General liability

54. _____ is NOT an advantage of Network Analysis

    A.   Simplifying the tasks of assessing the reliability of the plan
    B.   Planning the sequence of jobs and tasks
    C.   Interdependences between jobs or tasks
    D.   Determining the longest length of time that the project can be completed

55. The Owner may _____ terminate the Contract for the Owner's convenience and without cause.

    A.   Within twenty-four hours of signing
    B.   Within forty-eight hours of signing
    C.   At any time
    D.   Not

56. Any person who commences any work before obtaining the necessary permits shall be subject to _____.

    A.   A fee equal to paying twice for improvements to your property
    B.   A fee equal to the required permit fees
    C.   A fee equal to 150% of the required permit fees
    D.   A fee established in addition to the required permit fees

57. _____ is a procedure under which progress billings are accelerated in relation to costs incurred.

    A.   Contract loading
    B.   Front end loading
    C.   Completed contract acceleration
    D.   Special completion treatment

58. Once the subcontractor is officially terminated, the contractor should _____.

    A.   Remove all the subcontractor's equipment and materials from the site
    B.   Leave all the subcontractor's equipment and materials on site until subcontractor's work is completed
    C.   Keep the materials to complete the work
    D.   Remove the subcontractor from the site and replace him with another subcontractor

59. One of the three C's of underwriting Bonds is NOT _____.

    A.   Capital
    B.   Character
    C.   Capacity
    D.   Contract

50. _____ shall be used in the absence of total agreement on the terms of a Change Order.

    A.   Unit pricing
    B.   A change directive
    C.   A construction change directive
    D.   A construction change order

51. The original contract amount is $252,134.00. The sum of the previous change orders was $12,125.00 and a third change has a value of $2,134.00 which includes a profit of $213.00. The new contract value would be _____.

    A. $266,606.00
    B. $267,213.00
    C. $266,393.00
    D. $266.933.00

52. The Bidder shall deliver the required bonds to the Owner not later than _____ hours following the execution of the Contract.

    A.   24
    B.   48
    C.   72
    D.   96

53. The required amount of property damage insurance coverage a general contractor will obtain and maintain is _____.

    A. $25,000
    B. $50,000
    C. $100,000
    D. $300,000

54. The Architect may order minor changes in the Work that are consistent with the intent of the Contract Documents and _____.

    A.   Does not have to be in writing
    B.   Shall be in writing
    C.   Shall be approved by the Owner
    D.   Does not have to be approved by the Owner

55. _____ contracts normally contain a ceiling price.

    A.   Fixed price
    B.   Lump sum
    C.   GMP
    D.   Cost plus

Please See Answer Key on following page

1 Exam Prep
Contract Administration
Practice Exam #4 Answers

<u>Answer</u>		<u>Reference</u>	<u>Section/Page#</u>

1.   B   OSHA   1926.102(c)(1)
Index: "Lenses - Eye protection"   Table E-1

2.   D   AIA Document A201, 2017   3.17
Index: "Copyrights and Patents"

3.   C   4 7/8' ÷ by 3/8" per foot or invert and multiply 39/8 x 8/3 = **13 ft**
Could also convert fractions to decimals
4 7/8 = 4.875 and 3/8 = .375, so 4.875 / .375 = **13 ft**

4.   A   Florida Contractors Manual   2021: 9-39
Index: Lien – "Final payment affidavit"   2017: 9-38

5.   C   Florida Contractors Manual   2021: 9-18
Index: "Lien – Priority"   2017: 9-17

6.   A   General Math – Pythagorean

Take diagonal

42'

74'

The length of the diagonal will be $a^2 + b^2 = c^2$ to ensure the formwork is square

$42^2 + 74^2 = c^2$ $1764ft^2 + 5476ft^2 = c^2$ therefore c = the square root of 7240 ft^2

c = 85.088 ft or convert to ft and inches – 85 + .088 ft (12in per ft) = 85'-1"

7.   D   Florida Building Code – Energy Conservation   R303.1.1.2.1
Index: Insulation – Installation

8.   C   Florida Building Code   105.2.1
Index: Permits

9.   A   Florida Contractors Manual   2021: 2-78
Index: "Qualifying Agent"   2017: 2-88
     §489.1195

10.   B   Florida Contractor Manual   2021/2017: 5-54
2021 TOC: "Workers Compensation Law"
2017 Index: "Acts – Worker's Compensation"

Answer		Reference	Section/Page#
11.	B	Florida Contractors Manual Index: "Environmental Compliance"	2017 – 10-97
12.	A	AIA Document A401, 2017 TOC: "Chapter 5 - Changes in Work"	5.3
13.	C	Florida Contractors Manual Index: "Licensing – Money received"	2021: 2-79 2017: 2-90 §489.126(2)(a)
14.	C	Florida Contractors Manual Index: "Lien – Claim of lien"	2021: 9-31 2017: 9-30
15.	D	AIA Document A201, 2017 Index: "Liens"	2.1.2
16.	D	Florida Contractors Manual Index: "Licensing – Local Governments"	2021: 2-111, 2-173 2017: 2-133, 2-199 §61G4-20.001(3) §489.531(4)(b)
17.	B	AIA Document A701, 2018 TOC: "Chapter 3 – Bidding Documents"	3.4.3
18.	C	Florida Contractors Manual 2021 TOC: Statute 713: 9-68 – "Notice of Termination" 2017 Index: "Lien – Notice of Termination"	2021: 9-79 2017: 9-91
19.	D	Florida Contractors Manual Index: "Cost Control"	10-70
20.	D	AIA Document A201, 2017 Index: Observations, Contractor – TOC: Chapter 3 – Contractor"	3.7.4
21.	B	Florida Contractors Manual Chapter 10 Definitions	10-73
22.	D	Florida Contractors Manual Index: "Scheduling and Guidelines"	10-63
23.	D	Walker's Building Estimator's Reference Book	32nd Ed: 471 31st Ed: 788

Flat area of the roof = 68 ft x 62.5 ft = 4,250 ft^2
Roof multiplier for 5/12 roof is 1.302
Estimated area to be roofed = 4.250 ft x 1.302 = 5,533.50 ft^2
Number of squares – one square will cover 100 ft^2
5,533.50 ft^2 / 100 ft^2 in a square = 55.335 squares

Answer		Reference	Section/Page#

24.   C   AIA Document A201, 2017   11.5.2
Index: "Insured Loss, Adjustment and Settlement of"

25.   C   Florida Contractors Manual   8-13
Index: "Scheduling – Float"

26.   D   Florida Contractors Manual   3-83

Total contract minus the amount previously received
$1,380,200 - $987,300 = $392,900 minus the amount being held for retainage
$392,900 - $138,020 = $254,880
After punch list is complete, retainage of $138,020 would be paid

27.   D   Florida Contractors Manual   2021: 2-158
Index: "Licensing – Penalties   2017: 2-184

28.   C   AIA Document A201, 2017   9.4.2
Index: "Certificate of Payment"

29.   C   Walker's Building Estimator's Reference Book   32nd Ed: 763
                                                         31st Ed: 1244

Slope = Rise / Run

Rise - Convert inches to feet – 8"/12" = .67'
Slope = .67' / 90' = .0074

30.   B   Florida Contractors Manual   2021: 9-12
Index: "Notices - Notice of Commencement"   2017: 9-11

31.   D   Florida Building Code   105.4.1
Index: "Permits"

32.   B   Walker's Building Estimator's Reference Book   32nd Ed: 763
                                                         31st Ed: 1244

% Grade = Slope x 100%

Slope = Rise / Run
Risc - Convert inches to feet – 8"/12" = .67'
Slope =.67' / 90' = .0074
% Grade = .0074 x 100% = .74%

33.   C   Florida Contractors Manual   3-80
Index: "Completed Contract"

Answer		Reference	Section/Page#

34. C Walker's Building Estimator's Reference Book

32nd Ed: 376 / 379
31st Ed: 633 / 636

Board feet = width (in) x thickness (in) x length (ft) / 12
Plates = 47 ft + 2(47 ft) = 141 ft
2 x 4 x 141 / 12 = 94 bdft
Studs = length in feet / spacing in feet plus 1
Spacing in feet = 16" / 12" = 1.33 ft
Studs = 47 ft / 1.33 ft = 35.34 round up to 36 and add 1 = 37 studs
Studs = 37 x 2 x 4 x 8 /12 = 197.33 bdft
Total = 291.33 bdft

35. A Florida Contractors Manual
Index: "Subcontractors"

10-68

36. D Walker's Building Estimator's Reference Book

32nd Ed: 348
31st Ed: 595

37. B Florida Contractors Manual
Index: Completed Contract

2021: 3-59
2021: 3-59

38. C Florida Contractors Manual
Index: Estimating – Labor & Manpower

10-30, 10-31

39. C Florida Building Code

303.1.2

40. B Florida Contractors Manual
Index: Inventory

3-80

41. D Florida Contractors Manual
2021 TOC: "Plans and Specifications – CSI Masterformat"
2017 Index: "CSI Masterformat"

2021: 10-6
2017: 10-7

42. B Florida Contractors Manual
2021 TOC: "Plans and Specifications – CSI Masterformat"
2017 Index: "CSI Masterformat"

2021: 10-6
2017: 10-7

43. C AIA Document A201
Index: "Claims, Notice of"

15.1.3.1

44. C Florida Contractors Manual
Index: "Qualifying Agent"

2021: 2-22
2017: 2-20

45. B AIA Document A401, 2017
TOC: "Chapter 11 – Payments"

11.1.3

Answer		Reference	Section/Page#
46.	C	Florida Contractors Manual Index: "Licensing – Changes in Information"	2021: 2-133 2017: 2-159 §61G4-15.007(1)
47.	C	AIA Document A201, 2017 Index: "Change Orders"	7.1.2
48.	C	Florida Contractors Manual Index: "Production Efficiency"	2021: 10-32 2017: 10-32
49.	C	Florida Building Code, Accessibility TOC: "Parking Spaces" – 2% of total = 1,000 x 2% = 20 spaces	Table 208.2
50.	A	AIA Document A201, 2017 Index: Architect, Extent of Authority"	4.2.3 / 4.2.7
51.	A	Florida Contractors Manual Index: "Licensing – Death of a Contractor"	2021: 2-78 2017: 2-89
52.	B	Florida Building Code Index: "Elevators – Emergency Operations"	[F] 3003.2
53.	A	Florida Contractors Manual Index: "Insurance"	4-7
54.	D	Florida Contractors Manual 2021 Index: "Scheduling – Network Analysis" 2017 Index: "Network Analysis"	2021: 2-57 2017: 2-57
55.	C	AIA Document A201, 2017 Index: Termination by Owner for Convenience"	14.4.1
56.	D	Florida Building Code Index: "Permits – fees"	[A] 109.4
57.	B	Florida Contractors Manual Definitions Chapter 10	2021: 10-73 2017: 10-74
58.	B	Florida Contractors Manual Index: "Subcontractors"	10-69
59.	D	Florida Contractors Manual Index: "Bonds – Three C's of underwriting"	4-15
60.	C	AIA Document A201, 2017 Index: "Construction Change Directive"	7.3.2

Answer		**Reference**	**Section/Page#**
61.	C	Original contract amount + change orders = New contract amount $252,134.00 + $12,125.00 + $2,134.00 = $266,393.00	
62.	C	AIA Document A701, 2018 TOC: "Bonds"	7.2.1
63.	B	Florida Contractors Manual Index: "Licensing – Public Liability Insurance"	2021: 2-16, 2-131 2017: 2-19, 2-157 §61G4.15.003
64.	B	AIA Document A201, 2017 Index: Minor change in the work"	7.4
65.	D	Florida Contractors Manual Index: "Types of Contracts "	2021: 8-7 2017: 8-8

Project Management
Practice Test 1

1. A contractor is to backfill a ditch that measures 14 ft x 24 ft by 4.5 ft deep. The soil compaction rate is 25%. The amount of soil required for this ditch is _____ cubic yards. Select the closest answer.

   A. 70
   B. 60
   C. 50
   D. 40

2. Lifelines in areas subjected to cutting or abrasion shall be a minimum of _____ inch wire core manila rope.

   A. 3/4
   B. 7/8
   C. 15/16
   D. 1/2

3. All excavations made in sandy loam soil 20 feet or less in depth which have vertically sided lower portions shall be shielded or supported to a height _____ inches above the top of the vertical side.

   A. At least 18
   B. A minimum of 16
   C. 12
   D. None of the above. Vertically sided lower portions in such excavations are not permitted

4. The calculated fire-resistance rating for a 3.8-inch-thick sand light weight aggregate precast concrete wall shall be _____ hour(s).

   A. 1
   B. 2
   C. 3
   D. 4

5. _____ shall be installed before using an aerial lift on an incline.

   A. Body belts
   B. Wheel chocks
   C. Lift controls
   D. Stabilizer jacks

6. When the rope is to be used for hositing or supporting personnel, a safety factor of _____ must be used.

    A. 5
    B. 10
    C. 15
    D. 20

7. High-density R-30 batt insulation used in cathedral ceilings are _____ inches thick.

    A. 8 ¼
    B. 8 ¾
    C. 9 ½
    D. 10

8. According to ASTM C94, when truck mixers are used the load must be completely discharged within _____ after batching.

    A. 1 hour
    B. 2 hours
    C. 45 minutes
    D. 90 minutes

9. Girders and beams at columns connections shall be closely fitted around columns and adjoining ends shall be _____ tied to each other.

    A. Cross
    B. Diagonally
    C. Horizontally
    D. Vertically

10. The thickness of concrete floor slabs supported directly on the ground shall not be less than _____ inches.

    A. 3 - 1/2
    B. 4
    C. 4 1/2
    D. 5

11. In high-velocity hurricane zones, electrical conduit, mechanical piping or any other service lines running on the roof shall be raised not less than _____ inches above the finished roof surface.

    A. 6
    B. 8
    C. 10
    D. 12

12. The maximum permissible slope for access aisles serving accessible parking spaces shall not be greater than _____ .

    A. 1 in 36
    B. 1 in 42
    C. 1 in 48
    D. 1 in 60

13. Excavations located five feet or less from the street lot line during the renovation of an existing building shall be enclosed with a barrier not less than _____ feet high.

    A. 8
    B. 5
    C. 7
    D. 6

14. Townhouses not more than three stories in height may be separated by a single wall providing such wall shall provide not less than a _____ hour fire resistance rating.

    A. 1
    B. 2
    C. 3
    D. 4

15. Spiral stairways shall be constructed in such a way that the risers shall be sufficient to provide a minimum headroom of _____ .

    A. 6'8"
    B. 7'6"
    C. 6'6"
    D. 5'10"

16. Whenever materials are dropped _____ to any point outside the exterior walls of the building, an enclosed chute shall be used.

    A. 20 feet
    B. 6 feet
    C. More than 20 feet
    D. 20 feet or less

17. Automatic sprinkler systems in residential structures up to and including four stories in height in buildings not exceeding 60 ft shall be permitted to be installed throughout in accordance with _____ .

    A. NFPA 13
    B. NFPA 13D
    C. NFPA 13R
    D. NFPA 101

18. Every portion of a floor that is more than _____ inches above the floor or grade below shall be provided with guards.

    A. 30
    B. 32
    C. 36
    D. 42

19. Fire walls shall be continuous from exterior wall to exterior wall and shall extend at least _____ inches beyond the exterior surface of exterior walls.

    A. 6
    B. 12
    C. 16
    D. 18

20. A single point adjustable scaffold consisting of a sling designed to support one employee is called a _____.

    A. Boatswains' chair
    B. Catenary scaffold
    C. Lean-to scaffold
    D. Shore scaffold

21. The minimum dimensions for a crawl space access opening in a building shall be not less than _____ inches.

    A. 24" x 32"
    B. 18" x 24"
    C. 20" x 30"
    D. 24" x 36"

22. A _____ truss develops movement at its bearing points when under load.

    A. Scissor
    B. Kingpost
    C. Bowstring
    D. Dual-Pitch

23. Excavated or other materials or equipment shall be effectively stored and retained at least _____ feet or more from the edge of the excavation.

    A. 2
    B. 3
    C. 4
    D. 5

24. Thermal bridging that occurs across steel framing members _____ the effectiveness of the insulation in the wall assembly.

    A. Increases
    B. Decreases
    C. Neither increases nor decreases
    D. Mitigates

25. Anchored stone veneer units not exceeding _____ inches in thickness shall be anchored directly to masonry, concrete or to stud construction.

    A. 6
    B. 8
    C. 10
    D. 12

26. Where the _____ of the soil is in doubt, the building official shall be permitted to require that a geotechnical investigation be conducted.

    A. Compressibility
    B. Granule size
    C. Water content
    D. All of the above

27. The maximum number of manually controlled jacks/lifting units used in lift-slab operations shall NOT exceed _____.

    A. 10
    B. 12
    C. 14
    D. 16

28. Do not remove Ground Bracing until all the Top Chord, Web and Bottom Chord Restraints and Braces are installed for at least the first _____ trusses.

    A. 5
    B. 10
    C. 12
    D. 8

29. Where oxygen deficiency or a hazardous atmosphere could be expected to exist, the atmosphere shall be tested before employees enter an excavation over _____ feet in depth.

    A. 2
    B. 4
    C. 5
    D. 6

30. Exposure to impulsive or impact noise should not exceed _____ db peak sound pressure level.

    A. 90
    B. 100
    C. 115
    D. 140

31. For shotcrete, the minimum size of reinforcement shall be No. _____ bars.

    A. 3
    B. 4
    C. 5
    D. 6

32. The maximum staple spacing for attaching 5/8-inch gypsum board to wood-framed wall assemblies having an allowable shear value of 175 plf shall be _____ inches.

    A. 4
    B. 5
    C. 6
    D. 7

33. Crickets and saddles are used to _____ .

    A. Divert water away from dormers
    B. Divert water away from the chimney
    C. Provide counterflashing on a roof edge
    D. Provide counterflashing on a roof valley

34. Signs identifying the location of accessible parking spaces shall be placed at least _____.

    A. 4 feet above the finished floor or ground surface measured to the bottom of the sign
    B. 5 feet above the finished floor or ground surface measured to the bottom of the sign
    C. 4 feet above the finished floor or ground surfaces measured to the top of the sign
    D. 5 feet above the finished floor or ground surface measured to the top of the sign

35. Minimum size lumber used as Lateral Restraint and Diagonal Bracing is _____ stress-graded lumber.

    A. 2 x 4
    B. 2 x 6
    C. 2 x 8
    D. 2 x 10

36. The maximum angle of repose for an excavation less than 20 feet deep in sand shall be _____ degrees.

    A. 90
    B. 34
    C. 45
    D. 53

37. When hoisting bundles of reinforcing bars roughly _____ feet or longer it may be necessary to use a spreader beam.

   A. 15
   B. 30
   C. 45
   D. 55

38. In shotcrete construction, the minimum clearance between parallel reinforcing bars #5 or smaller shall be not less than _____ inches.

   A. 3
   B. 3 ½
   C. 2
   D. 2 ½

39. The occupant load per unit area for business is _____ gross.

   A. 50
   B. 100
   C. 120
   D. 150

40. All masonry walls over _____ feet in height shall be adequately braced.

   A. 4
   B. 6
   C. 8
   D. 10

41. The minimum number of exits that shall be provided for a two-story building with an occupant load of 750 per story is _____.

   A. 3
   B. 6
   C. 4
   D. 2

42. Floors in storage areas for Group H-2 and H-3 occupancies for organic peroxides, oxidizers and unstable materials and water reactive solids and liquids shall be of _____ construction.

   A. Liquid-tight, noncombustible
   B. Barricade
   C. Explosion venting
   D. Noncombustible

43. A _____ must be used if necessary to prevent rotation of the load that would be hazardous.

    A. Restriction line
    B. Tag Line
    C. Chain
    D. Control line

44. Clearance between wood siding and the earth on the exterior of a building shall not be less than _____ inches.

    A. 2
    B. 4
    C. 6
    D. 8

45. When crawl space is not vented to the outside, the wall shall be permitted to be insulated and all joints of the vapor retarder shall overlap by _____ inches and be sealed or taped.

    A. 2
    B. 4
    C. 6
    D. 8

46. Oily rags shall be kept in a _____ until removed from the worksite.

    A. Fire-resistant covered container
    B. Storage drum
    C. Metal garbage can with cover
    D. None of the above. Oily rags should be removed from the jobsite weekly

47. If a project is not located in Northwest Florida, the application for a permit for new stormwater discharge would be submitted to the _____ .

    A. FDEP
    B. Water Management District
    C. Building Department
    D. Army Core of Engineers

48. Combustible materials shall be permitted in _____ construction.

    A. Type I and Type II
    B. Type III
    C. Type IV
    D. Type V

49. Where handrails are not continuous between flights, the handrails shall extend horizontally not less than 12 inches beyond the top riser and continue to slope for the depth of _____ beyond the bottom riser.

    A. 6 inches
    B. 12 inches
    C. One tread
    D. One riser

50. Gravel or slag on built-up roofs provides _____.

    A. Protection
    B. Waterproofing
    C. Insulation
    D. Slip and fall protection

51. During lift-slab operations employing multiple jacks, all points at which the slab is supported shall be kept _____.

    A. Within ¼ inch of level
    B. Within ½ inch of level
    C. Within ¾ inch of level
    D. Level

52. The required capacity of each door opening shall have a minimum clear width of _____ inches.

    A. 32
    B. 34
    C. 36
    D. 42

53. For trusses over 60 ft, the spreader bar prevents lateral bending and should be attached to the Top Chords and Webs at _____ feet intervals.

    A. 6
    B. 8
    C. 10
    D. 12

54. Deformations on rebar _____.

    A. Provide information about the bar's strength and place of manufacture
    B. Improve its strength
    C. Are standard
    D. Increase the volume of the steel and contribute to the strength of the resulting structure

55. Concrete mixers with _____ cyd or larger loading skips shall be equipped with mechanical devices to clear the skip of materials and guardrails installed on each side of the skip.

    A. ½
    B. 1
    C. 1 ½
    D. 2

56. Ground bracing connections should use a minimum of _____ nails clinched unless otherwise specified.

    A. 2 – 10d
    B. 2 – 12d
    C. 2 – 16d
    D. 3 – 16d

57. Glass block panels shall be provided with expansion joints along _____ at all structural supports.

    A. The top and bottom
    B. Both sides
    C. The top and sides
    D. The top, bottom and both sides

58. It is critical to install temporary Lateral Restraint and Diagonal Bracing for the Top Chord and Web Member Plane immediately to prevent _____ of the Truss.

    A. Out-of-plane buckling
    B. Improper alignment
    C. Excessive deflection
    D. Improper spacing

59. The maximum screw spacing for 5/8 gypsum board installed perpendicular to wood framing on the ceiling shall be _____ inches.

    A. 7
    B. 12
    C. 16
    D. 24

60. Foundation walls of rough or random rubble stone shall not be less than _____ inches thick.

    A. 12
    B. 32
    C. 16
    D. 24

61. When masonry blocks are stacked higher than 6 feet, _____.

    A. Mechanical equipment shall be used to stack the blocks
    B. The stack shall be tapered back one-half block per tier above the 6-foot level
    C. The stack shall be located no less than 6 feet from the structure
    D. None of the above. Masonry blocks shall not be stacked higher than 6 feet

62. Recordable incidents must be entered within _____ days of learning of its occurrence.

    A. Five
    B. Five working days
    C. Seven
    D. Seven working days

63. When using screws to install gypsum panels to wood framing, the screws shall penetrate the underlying wood not less than _____ inch.

    A. 3/8
    B. 7/16
    C. 7/8
    D. 5/8

64. The R-value of insulation for a cathedral ceiling is _____.

    A. R-19
    B. R-30
    C. R-38
    D. R-25

65. Permanent platforms in Type IV construction are permitted to be constructed of fire-retardant-treated wood where the platforms are _____.

    A. Not more than ¼ of the room area
    B. Not more than 3600 square feet in area
    C. Not more than 30 inches above the main floor
    D. Above a space used only for storage

Please see Answer Key on following page

ALH 02/15/2022

Project Management
Practice Test 1
Answer Key

CM: Florida Contractors Manual

A201, A401, A701: Various AIA documents

FBC: FL Building Code; Building/Residential/Existing Building/Energy Conservation/ Accessibility

Walker's: Walker's Building Estimator's Reference Book

OSHA: 29 CFR 1926 OSHA Construction Industry Regulations

PPCC: Principles and Practices of Commercial Construction

DCCM: Design and Control of Concrete Mixtures

Rebar: Placing Reinforcing Bars

EEBC: Energy Efficient Building Construction in Florida

Truss: BCSI Guide to Good Practice for handling, Installing, Restraining & Bracing of Metal Plate Connected Wood Trusses

TOC: Table of Contents

No.	Answer	Book and page (Location)
1	A	14 ft x 24 ft x 4.5 ft= 1,512 cft x 1.25% compaction rate = 1,890 cft - convert to cyd– 1,890 cft / 27 cft per cyd = 70 cyd Trade Knowledge
2	B	OSHA, sect. 1926.104(c). (Index: "Lifelines – See Fall Protection")
3	A	OSHA, sect. 1926 Subpart P Appendix B – Sloping and Benching - Fig. B-1.2 – condition (3) ------ to identify soil as Type B (Index: "Soil Classification for Excavations")
4	B	FBC- Building Table 722.2.1.1 (Index: "Fire Resistance, Calculated")
5	B	OSHA, sect. 1926.453 (b)(2)(vii) (Index: "Aerial Lifts")
6	B	CM, pg. 7-53. (Index: "Rope – Safety Factor")
7	A	EEBC, 10th Ed. pg. 122; EEBC, 9th Ed. pg. 120
8	D	Trade Knowledge - PPCC – 9th edition pg. 230 – 10th edition pg. 233 – (Index: "Mixer – Concrete") and DCCM – pg. 400/473 (Index: "Mixing Concrete")
9	A	FBC-Building, sect. 2304.11.1.1 (Index: "Wood, Wall Framing")
10	A	FBC-Building, sect. 1907.1 (Index: "Concrete, Slab, minimum or Slab on ground, concrete")
11	B	FBC-Building, Sec: 1522.3.4 (TOC: Chap 15 "Roof Assemblies and Rooftop Structures and Components – High Velocity Hurricane Zones – Rooftop Structures and Components")
12	C	FBC- Accessibility sect. 502.4, Exception. (TOC: Chapter 5 "Parking Spaces")
13	D	FBC-Building sect. 3306.9 (Index: "Barriers, Pedestrian protection)
14	B	FBC-Building, Sect 706.4.1.2(1) (Index: "Fire Walls" and TOC: Chap 7 "Fire and Smoke Protection Features – Fire Walls")
15	C	FBC-Building, sect:1011.3, 1011.10 (Index: "Spiral Stairways, Construction")
16	C	OSHA, sect. 1926.252(a) (Index: "Chutes – Waste Disposal")
17	C	FBC-Building, sect. [F]903.3.1.2 (Index: "Sprinkler System, Automatic")
18	A	FBC- Building, sect. 1015.2 (Index: "Guards")
19	D	FBC-Building, sect 706.5 (Index: "Fire Walls – Continuity")
20	A	OSHA, sect. 1926.450 (Index: "Scaffolds - definitions")

21	B	FBC-Building, sect. 1209.1 (Index: "Crawl Space, Access and Access Openings, Crawl Space")
22	A	Walker's, (32nd Ed.) Pg. 394 (31st Ed.) Pg. 656. (Index: "Trusses, Wood roof.")
23	A	OSHA, sect. 1926.651 (j) (2) (Index: "Excavations ")
24	B	EEBC, 10th Ed. pg. 114; EEBC, 9th Ed. pg. 112 (Index: "Insulation – of steel framed walls")
25	C	FBC-Building, sect 1405.7 (Index: "Stone Veneer")
26	A	FBC-Building, sect.1803.5.2 (Index: "Soils and Foundations, Geotechnical investigation")
27	C	OSHA, sect. 1926.705(j) (Index: "Jacks, Lift slab concrete construction operations or Lift Slab Construction or Concrete Construction, Lift-slab operations")
28	A	BCSI, pg. 20. (TOC. "Summary of the Eight- Steps in the Truss Installation Process")
29	B	OSHA, sect. 1926.651 (g) (1) (i) (Index: "Excavations – Hazardous Atmospheres")
30	D	OSHA, sect. 1926.52 (c) (Index: "Noise Exposure")
31	C	FBC-Building, sect 1908.4.1 (Index: "Shotcrete")
32	A	FBC-Building, Table 2306.3(3) (Index: "Gypsum, Fastening")
33	B	Trade Knowledge
34	B	FBC-Accessibility, sect. 502.6.1 (TOC: Chapter 5 "Parking Spaces")
35	A	BCSI, pg. 10. (TOC: "Restraint/Bracing Material & Connections")
36	B	OSHA, Sec. 1926 Subpart P Appendix A (to identify "sand" as a "Type C" soil), and Sub part P Appendix B, Table B-1 for maximum allowable slopes. (Index: "Soil Classification for Excavations")
37	B	Trade Knowledge – Rebar pg. 8-7
38	D	FBC-Building, sect. 1908.4.2 (Index: "Shotcrete")
39	D	FBC-Building, Table 1004.5 (Index: "Occupant Load – Determination of")
40	C	OSHA, sect. 1926.706 (b). (Index: "Masonry")
41	B	FBC-Building, 2017 Table 1006.3.1 and 2020 Table 1006.3.2 (Index: "Exit, Number, minimum")
42	A	FBC-Building, [F] 415.8.4 (TOC: "Chapter 4 – Special Detailed Requirements Based on Occupancy and Use – Groups H-1, H-2, H-3, H-4 and H-5")
43	B	OSHA, sect. 1926.1417 (w) (Index: "Tag Lines")
44	C	FBC-Building, sect. 2304.12.1.5 (Index: "Wood – contacting: concrete, masonry or earth")
45	C	FBC-Energy Conservation, sect. R402.2.11 (Index: Insulation: Crawl space walls")
46	A	OSHA, sect. 1926.252 (e) (Index; "Disposal, Waste Materials")
47	B	CM pg. 10-93 (Index: "Environmental Compliance")
48	D	FBC-Building, sect: 602.5 (Index: "Combustible Material – Type I and Type II")
49	C	FBC-Building, sect: 1014.6 (Index: "Handrails, Extensions")
50	A	Trade Knowledge – PPCC – 10th on pg. 480 and 9th ed on pg. 416 (Index: "Built-up roofing membrane roofs)
51	B	OSHA, sect. 1926.705(g) (Index: "Lift-slab Construction")
52	A	FBC-Building, sect. 1010.1.1 (Index: "Doors - width") and FBC – Accessibility, (Figure 404.2.3 "Clear Width of Doorways")
53	C	BCSI, pg. 9. (TOC. "Mechanical Hoisting Recommendations for Single Trusses")
54	C	Rebar, 9th edition 6-1 and Rebar 10th edition 7-1
55	B	OSHA, sect. 1926.702(b)(1) &(b)(2). (Index: "Concrete Construction, Equipment and tools")
56	C	BCSI, pg. 10 Figure B1-17 (TOC. "Ground Brace - Exterior")

57	C	FBC-Residential, sect. 607.7 (TOC, Chap 6: "R607 Glass Unit Masonry")
58	A	BCSI, pg. 12. (TOC: "Temporary Installation Restraint/Bracing Requirements...")
59	B	FBC – Residential, Table R702.3.5 (Index: "Gypsum")
60	C	FBC-Building, sect. 1807.1.3 (Index: "Concrete - Foundation Walls") FBC-Residential, sect. R404.1.8 (Index: "Concrete - Foundation Walls")
61	B	OSHA, sect. 1926.250(b)(7). (Index "Materials Storage")
62	C	CM, 2021 pg. 7-6; 2017 pg. 2-7 (Index "OSHA - Recordkeeping")
63	D	FBC – Residential, R702.3.5.1 (Index: "Gypsum")
64	B	EEBC, 10th Ed. pg. 1, Fig. 1-1 and page 122; EEBC, 9th Ed. pg. 1, Fig. 1-1 and page 120
65	C	FBC-Building, sect. 410.4 (Index: "Platform - Construction") (Index: "Fire Retardant Treated Wood – Platforms")

Project Management
Practice Test 2

1. A _____ inch inspection zone above grade is one of the key elements of energy efficient building construction.

    A. 2
    B. 4
    C. 6
    D. 8

2. Reinforcing bars meeting ASTM requirements with _____ are considered to be acceptable without cleaning or brushing.

    A. Machine oil
    B. Mud
    C. Rust
    D. Grease

3. A _____ level is the least expensive and most convenient instrument for use when building a wood deck.

    A. Laser
    B. Water bubble
    C. Transit
    D. Builders

4. The maximum framing spacing for ½ inch single layer gypsum ceiling board applied perpendicular to the framing shall be _____ inches.

    A. 12
    B. 16
    C. 24
    D. 30

5. A _____ crane is a piece of equipment that has a type of base mounting which incorporated a continuous belt of sprocket driven track.

    A. Tower
    B. Crawler
    C. Portal
    D. Mobile

6. Any portion of a masonry fireplace located within the exterior wall of a building shall have a clearance to combustibles of not less than _____ inches from the back faces of masonry fireplaces

    A. 2
    B. 3
    C. 4
    D. 5

7. If the contractor does not have access to details for truss installation, _____ would be contacted for the most current industry standards.

    A. ANSI
    B. NFBA
    C. SBCA
    D. ASCE

8. _____ inches is the approximate diameter of #5 rebar.

    A. .375
    B. .500
    C. .625
    D. .750

9. 1/25 inch is equal to approximately _____ mm.

    A. .50
    B. .74
    C. 1.00
    D. 1.25

10. Many project specifications require that discharge of concrete be completed within _____ minutes of mixing.

    A. 60
    B. 70
    C. 80
    D. 90

11. When using screws to install gypsum panel products to cold-formed steel framing, the screws shall penetrate the steel not less than _____ inch.

    A. 3/8
    B. 3/4
    C. 5/8
    D. 7/16

12. Solid wood doors have a U-factor of about _____.

    A. 0.30
    B. 0.40
    C. 0.50
    D. 0.70

13. A _____ test is the most generally accepted method used to measure the consistency of concrete.

    A. Density
    B. Slump
    C. Concrete.yield
    D. Water to cement ratio

14. Cutting or drilling truss members in the field shall not be done without the approval of the _____.

    A. Truss Manufacturer
    B. Building Inspector
    C. Engineer
    D. Architect

15. Where used, toeboards shall be capable of withstanding, without failure, a force of at least _____ pounds applied in any downward or horizontal direction at any point.

    A. 10
    B. 45
    C. 50
    D. 75

16. The minimum thickness of high density blown cellulose insulation providing an R-value of R-32 in attics is _____ inches.

    A. 5.1
    B. 6.5
    C. 8.6
    D. 10.8

17. The maximum Top Chord Temporary Lateral Restraint (TCTLR) spacing required for a 30' to 45' truss span is _____ feet on-center maximum.

    A. 4
    B. 6
    C. 8
    D. 10

18. Fasteners shall be spaced not more than _____ inch from the edges and ends of horizontal gypsum board or gypsum panel products used on diaphragm ceilings.

    A. ¼
    B. ½
    C. 3/8
    D. 7

19. The detail for rebar to be used on a project would be located _____.

    A. In the specifications
    B. On a civil drawing sheet
    C. On a structural drawing sheet
    D. On a project architectural sheet

20. Exterior cement plaster coats shall be protected from freezing for a period of not less than 24 hours after set has occurred and shall be applied when the ambient temperature is higher than _____ °F.

    A. 40
    B. 45
    C. 50
    D. 55

21. Level 3 alterations apply where the work area exceeds _____ percent.

    A. 20
    B. 30
    C. 40
    D. 50

22. Lifelines that may be subjected to cutting or abrasion shall be a minimum of _____ inch wire core manila rope.

    A. 1/2
    B. 3/4
    C. 1
    D. 7/8

23. The minimum net area of ventilation openings shall be not less than 1 square foot for each _____ square feet of under-floor crawl space area.

    A. 10
    B. 50
    C. 100
    D. 150

24. A _____ inch thick base course consisting of clean graded sand, gravel, crushed stone, crushed concrete or crushed blast-furnace slag passing a 2-inch sieve shall be placed on the prepared subgrade where the slab is below grade.

    A. 2
    B. 3
    C. 4
    D. 6

25. A _____ load is produced by use and occupancy of the building and other structures.

    A. Dead
    B. Live
    C. Structural
    D. Construction

26. Where oxygen deficiency or atmospheres containing less than 19.5% oxygen exists, the maximum excavation depth employees can enter without first testing the atmosphere shall be _____ feet.

    A. 4
    B. 3
    C. 6
    D. 5

27. Training for Class III asbestos work shall include at least _____ hours of "hands on" training.

    A. 2
    B. 8
    C. 14
    D. 16

28. All new safety nets shall meet accepted performance standards of _____ foot-pounds minimum impact resistance.

    A. 5,000
    B. 4,000
    C. 17,500
    D. 5,400

29. Fire-retardant-treated wood shall have when tested a listed flame spread index of _____ or less.

    A. 25
    B. 23
    C. 20
    D. 19

30. Soils shall be considered to be expansive if tests show that _____.

    A. It has a plasticity index less than 15
    B. More than 10% of the soil particles are more than 5 micrometers in size
    C. More than 10 % of the soil particles pass a No 200 sieve
    D. It has an expansion index greater than 2

31. In gravel, excavations 20' or less in depth shall have a maximum allowable slope of _____.

    A. 1:1
    B. ½:1
    C. 1 ½:1
    D. ¾: 1

32. Screws for attaching gypsum board and gypsum panel products to wood framing shall be _____ screws.

    A. Drywall
    B. Type W
    C. Wood
    D. Bugle head style

33. For floor or ground surfaces slopes not steeper than _____ shall be permitted.

    A. 1:12
    B. 1:36
    C. 1:40
    D. 1:48

34. Excavations made in _____ soil that are less than 12' deep and open short term, can have a maximum allowable slope of ½: 1.

    A. Type C
    B. Type A
    C. Type B
    D. Both Type A and Type C

35. _____ wheelchair spaces shall be provided for a food establishment with fixed seating capacity for 70 people.

    A. 2
    B. 3
    C. 4
    D. 5

36. When the manufacturer does not specify plumb tolerance, tower cranes must be plumb to a tolerance of at least _____ inch to 40 feet.

    A. ½
    B. ¾
    C. 1
    D. 1 ½

37. Coarse aggregate, if used, in shotcrete construction shall not exceed _____ inch.

    A. ¼
    B. ½
    C. 5/8
    D. ¾

38. The employer must provide each employee with head protection that meets the specifications set forth by _____ standards.

    A. UL
    B. ASTM
    C. ANSI
    D. OSHA

39. The minimum cover for reinforcement in concrete cast in removable forms that will be exposed to the earth or weather shall be _____ inches for No 5 bars and smaller.

    A. ¾
    B. 1 ½
    C. 3
    D. 2

40. Specially designed slotted metal clips that can be used to hold trusses in alignment and allow for seasonal movement are known as _____ connections.

    A. Conventional
    B. Floating
    C. Anchorage
    D. Toe-nailing

41. The type of machines and tools that would usually require point of operation guarding is _____.

    A. Portable power tools
    B. Alligator shears
    C. Forming rolls and calendars
    D. All of the above

42. The minimum diameter of hoisting and counterweight wire ropes shall be _____ inch

    A. 5/8
    B. 7/8
    C. 1/2
    D. 3/4

43. A cull means _____.

    A. Rejected
    B. Approved
    C. Acceptable
    D. Standard

44. Handrails in a townhouse stairway shall not project more than _____ inches on either side of the stairway.

    A. 4
    B. 4 ½
    C. 4 ¾
    D. 5

45. The latest generation surveying instruments are _____.

    A. Self-leveling
    B. Self-reading
    C. Self-leveling and self-reading
    D. None of the above

46. Deformed steel reinforcing bar is considered _____.

    A. Rejected
    B. Replaceable
    C. Acceptable
    D. Standard

47. The minimum size of a window used for an emergency escape shall have a minimum net clear opening of _____ ft^2.

    A. 5.7
    B. 6.2
    C. 5
    D. 4

48. When calculating total fire resistance ratings, the time assigned for 1/2-inch Type X gypsum wallboard applied to the fire-exposed side of a wall shall be _____ minutes.

    A. 15
    B. 20
    C. 25
    D. 40

49. Compressed air shall NOT be used for cleaning purposes except where reduced to less than _____ psi and then only with effective chip guarding and personal protective equipment.

    A. 30
    B. 40
    C. 50
    D. 100

50. All haulage vehicles whose pay load is loaded by means of cranes, power shovels, loaders or similar equipment shall _____.

    A. Have anchored supports to equalize the load
    B. Have a power rating equal to 4x the average load
    C. Have a cab shield /canopy to protect the operator
    D. Have a unibody chassis

51. Fireblocking shall be provided in concealed spaces between _____.

    A. Stair stringers at the top and bottom of the run
    B. Wood in roof construction, including girders, trusses, framing, and decking
    C. Stairwells in two story buildings of Type I and IA construction
    D. Nonbearing partitions where the required fire-resistance rating is 2 hours or less

52. _____ improve the workability of concrete.

    A. Accelerators
    B. Polymers
    C. Air-entraining admixtures
    D. Retarding admixtures

53. The width of a hallway shall be not less than _____ inches.

    A. 30
    B. 36
    C. 42
    D. 44

54. Trusses greater than 30 ft. in length require the use of _____ when being hoisted.

    A. A spreader bar
    B. A stiff back
    C. Diagonal bracing
    D. Two pick points

55. A 6-mil polyethylene vapor retarder with joints lapped not less than _____ inches shall be placed between the base course or subgrade and the concrete floor slab.

    A. 3
    B. 6
    C. 4
    D. 2

56. When masonry blocks are stacked higher than _____ feet, the stack shall be tapered back one-half block per tier above this level.

    A. 2
    B. 4
    C. 6
    D. 7

57. Handrails with a circular cross section shall have an outside diameter not greater than _____ inches.

    A. ¾
    B. 1 ¼
    C. 1 ¾
    D. 2

58. The skylight area in commercial buildings shall not be greater than _____ percent of the gross roof area.

    A. 1
    B. 2
    C. 3
    D. 5

59. Slump in concrete placed in removable forms shall not exceed _____ inches.

    A. 3
    B. 4
    C. 5
    D. 6

60. All pneumatically driven nails, staplers, and other similar equipment provided with automatic fastener feed, which operates at more than _____ psi pressure at the tool shall have a safety device on the muzzle to prevent the tool from ejecting fasteners unless the muzzle is in contact with the work surface.

    A. 50
    B. 100
    C. 75
    D. 30

61. When trusses are designed to bear directly on top of a structural wood support, toe-nailing the truss chord to the support is typically required to resist _____.

    A. Uplift
    B. Lateral forces
    C. Longitudinal forces
    D. Both A and B

62. The maximum permissible span for a nominal 2x10 wood plank with a maximum intended load of 50 psf shall be _____ feet.

    A. 6
    B. 8
    C. 4
    D. 10

63. Thresholds, if provided at doorways, shall be _____ inch high maximum.

    A. ½
    B. ¼
    C. ¾
    D. 5/8

64. When portable ladders are used for access to an upper landing surface, the ladder side rails shall extend at least _____ feet above the upper landing surface to which the ladder is used to gain access.

    A. 1
    B. 2
    C. 3
    D. 4

65. A company with a safety program in place should conduct jobsite safety inspections _____.

    A. Weekly
    B. Monthly
    C. Twice a week
    D. Daily

Please see Answer Key on the following page

4/26/22

Project Management
Practice Test 2
Answer Key

CM: Florida Contractors Manual

A201, A401, A701: Various AIA documents

FBC: FL Building Code; Building/Residential/Existing Building/Energy Conservation/ Accessibility

Walker's: Walker's Building Estimator's Reference Book

OSHA: 29 CFR 1926 OSHA Construction Industry Regulations

PPCC: Principles and Practices of Commercial Construction

DCCM: Design and Control of Concrete Mixtures

Rebar: Placing Reinforcing Bars

EEBC: Energy Efficient Building Construction in Florida

Truss: BCSI Guide to Good Practice for handling, Installing, Restraining & Bracing of Metal Plate Connected Wood Trusses

TOC: Table of Contents

No.	Answer	Book and page (Location)
1	C	EEBC 10th Ed. pg. 1, Figure 1-1; EEBC 9th Ed. pg. 1, Figure 1-1
2	C	Trade Knowledge – Rebar 9th and 10th edition – pg. 8-2 to 8-3
3	B	Trade Knowledge
4	C	FBC Residential, Table R702.3.5 (Index: "Gypsum")
5	B	OSHA, sect. 1926.1401 Definitions (Index: "Cranes")
6	C	FBC-Building, Sect. 2111.12 (Index: "Fireplaces, Masonry – Combustibles")
7	C	BCSI pg. 99 Reference (TOC: "Industry Standards")
8	C	Trade Knowledge – size # / 8 = diameter – Rebar – 9th edition p 6-2/ 10th edition 7-1
9	C	CM pg. 10-90 (Index: "Metric Conversions")
10	D	Trade Knowledge - DCCM - 16th Ed. Pg. 473 - 17th Ed. Pg. 393 (Index: "Transporting Concrete")
11	A	FBC Residential, section R702.3.5.1 (Index: "Gypsum")
12	C	EEBC, 10th Ed. pg. 153; EEBC, 9th Ed. pg. 152 (Index: "Doors - UFactor")
13	B	DCCM 16th Ed. Pg. 506 - 17th Ed. Pg. 428 (Index: "Testing freshly mixed concrete" - "consistency")
14	A	BCSI pgs. 55 (TOC: "Truss Damage")
15	C	OSHA sect. 1926.451 (h)(4)(i) (Index: "Scaffolds, Fall protection and Toeboards, Scaffolds")
16	C	EEBC, 10th Ed. pg. 118, Table 6-5; EEBC, 9th Ed. pg. 116, Table 6-5 (Index: "Insulation – of attic floors")
17	C	BCSI pg. 12 (TOC: "Temporary Restraint") Table B1-4, or pg. 21 – Step 2: Table B2-1
18	C	FBC-Building, sect. 2508.5.4 (2017), sect. 2508.6.4 (2020) – (Index: "Gypsum – Fastening"
19	C	Trade Knowledge – can be found in Walkers, (32nd Ed.) Pg. 27 (31st Ed.) Pg. 55
20	A	FBC-Building, sect. 2512.4 – (TOC: "Gypsum – Plaster - Exterior")
21	D	FBC- Existing 2017, Sect. 505.1 (TOC: "Chapter 5 – Classification of Work") FBC - Existing 2020, Sect. 605.1 (TOC: Chapter 6 – Classification of Work")
22	D	OSHA, sect. 1926.104 (c). (Index: "Lifelines – see Fall Protection")

23	D	FBC- Building sect. 1203.4.1. (Index: "Ventilation – Crawl space") and (Index: "Crawl Space – Ventilation")
24	C	FBC – Residential, sect. R506.2.2 – (Index: "Concrete - Floors on ground")
25	B	FBC-Building, (Index: "Loads – Live")
26	A	OSHA sect. 1926.651 (g) (1) (i). (Index: "Excavation – Hazardous Atmosphere")
27	D	OSHA sect. 1926.1101 (k) (9) (v). (Index: "Training - Asbestos")
28	C	OSHA sect. 1926.105 (d). (Index: "Safety Nets, see Nets, Safety")
29	A	FBC-Building sect 2303.2. (Index: "Wood - Fire-retardant treated") and (Index: "Fire-Retardant-Treated Wood")
30	C	FBC-Building pg. sect. 1803.5.3 (Index: "Soils - Expansive")
31	C	OSHA sect. 1926.652 Subpart P Appendix B, Table B-1 (Index: ("Soil Classification and Excavations – Sloping and Benching") ------- to identify soil as Type C (Index: "Soil Classification for Excavations")
32	B	FBC – Residential, sect. R702.3.5.1 (Index: "Gypsum")
33	D	FBC – Accessibility sect. 305.2 exception
34	B	OSHA sect. 1926.652 Subpart P Appendix B, Table B-1.1 Excavation in Type A soil - note 1. exception (Index: "Excavations - Sloping and Benching.")
35	C	FBC-Accessibility Table 221.2.1.1 (TOC: Chap 2 "Assembly Areas")
36	C	OSHA sect. 1926.1435 (b) (5) (Index: "Cranes") Section Content above Section 1400 – Tower Cranes
37	D	FBC-Building, sect. 1908.3 (Index: "Shotcrete")
38	C	OSHA sect 1926.100 (Index: "Head Protection")
39	B	FBC – Residential, sect. R404.1.3.3.7.4 Tab - Concrete Cover
40	B	BCSI pg. 94 – Glossary of Terms
41	D	OSHA sect. 1926.300 (b) (4)(iv). (Index: "Tools, Hand and Power - Guarding")
42	C	OSHA sect. 1926.552 (c) (14) (ii). Index: ("Ropes, Wire – Hoists and Elevators.")
43	A	Trade Knowledge – Walker's (32nd Ed.) Pg. 888 (31st Ed.) 1424
44	B	FBC – Residential, sect. R311.7.1 (2017) and R311.7.8.5 (2020) (Index: "Stairways")
45	C	Trade Knowledge – PPCC – 9th edition pg. 24-29, 10th edition pg. 30
46	D	Trade Knowledge – Rebar 9th edition pg. 6-1, Rebar 10th edition pg. 7-1
47	A	FBC -Building, Sect - 1030.2 (Index: "Windows - Emergency Egress Openings")
48	C	FBC-Building, Table 722.2.1.4(2). (Index: "Gypsum - Fire Resistance")
49	A	OSHA sect. 1926.302 (b) (4). (Index: "Compressed Air, Pneumatic Power Tools")
50	C	OSHA sect. 1926.601(b)(6) (Index: "Motor Vehicles")
51	A	FBC-Building, sect. 718.2.4 (Index: "Fireblocking")
52	C	DCCM - 16th Ed. Pg. 210 Table 9-1. Concrete Admixtures by Classification (Index: *"Chemical admixtures" – "Accelerating"* 17th Ed. Pgs. 118 – 119, 130 Table 6-1. Concrete Admixtures by Classification (Index: *"Chemical admixtures" – "set-retarding"*)
53	B	FBC- Residential, sect. R311.6 (Index: "Hallways")
54	A	BCSI pg. 9 (TOC, "Mechanical Hoisting Recommendations for Single Trusses")
55	B	FBC-Building, sect. 1907.1. (Index: "Slab on Ground – Concrete or Concrete – slab, minimum")
56	C	OSHA sect 1926.250(b)(7) (Index: "Materials, Storage")
57	D	FBC-Building, 1014.3.1 (Index: "Handrails – Graspability")
58	C	FBC - Energy Conservation, sect C402.4.1 (Index: "Skylights, Maximum Area")
59	D	FBC – Residential, sect. R404.1.3.3.4 Tab – Slump

60	B	OSHA sect 1926.302(b)(3) (Index: "Pneumatic Power Tools")
61	D	BCSI pg. 64 (TOC: "Toe-Nailing Used with Bottom-Bearing Applications.")

62	A	OSHA, 1926.451 Subpart L, Appendix A – Scaffold Specifications – section 1(b)(i) – Table (Index: "Plank, Planking – scaffolding")
63	A	FBC-Accessibility sect 404.2.5 (TOC: Chap 4 "Doors, Doorways and Gates")
64	C	OSHA, sect 1926.1053 (b)(1). (Index: "Ladders")
65	D	CM pg. 7-38 (Index: "Safety Programs" and TOC: Chap 7 "Components of a Safety Program or "OSHA - Inspections")

Project Management
Practice Test 3

1. A good rule to estimate the weight of the bundle is to use _____ pounds per foot of truss length time the number of trusses in the bundle.

    A. 5
    B. 10
    C. 15
    D. 20

2. Supply and return ducts in attics shall be insulated to a minimum of _____ where 3 inches in diameter and greater.

    A. R- 6
    B. R- 8
    C. R- 4
    D. R- 4.2

3. Excavations shall be sloped at an angle not steeper than _____ unless designed by a registered professional engineer.

    A. 34⁰
    B. 45⁰
    C. 53⁰
    D. 65⁰

4. The approximate solar heat gain coefficient (SHGC) for double-glazed windows with ¼ inch tinted glass is _____.

    A. .67
    B. .70
    C. .76
    D. .58

5. Trusses should not be installed with a maximum bow in any chord or panel exceeding _____.

    A. 1/4 inch of the plan dimensions
    B. 1/50 of the depth
    C. ½ inch
    D. 2 inches

6. For power lines rated 50 kV or below, the minimum clearance distance between the lines and any part of a crane or load shall be _____ feet.

   A. 6
   B. 10
   C. 15
   D. 20

7. A SEER of 14 means the unit provides _____ Btu's of cooling per watt-hour of electricity.

   A. 7
   B. 12
   C. 14
   D. 28

8. Crawl spaces shall be provided with not fewer than one access opening that shall be not less than _____.

   A. 18" x 24"
   B. 16" x 36"
   C. 20" x 30"
   D. 22" x 36"

9. The R-value of R-11 insulation compressed 60% of its original thickness shall be ___.

   A. R-10
   B. R-9
   C. R-8
   D. R-7

10. When installing gypsum panel products on a ceiling that will support insulation and will have a water-based texture finish, which of the following conditions is acceptable when the supporting framing is spaced 24 inches on-center?

   A. 3/8-inch panels applied perpendicular to framing
   B. ½-inch panels applied parallel to framing
   C. ½-inch panels applied perpendicular to framing
   D. 5/8-inch panels applied perpendicular to framing

11. 600 mm is approximately _____ inches.

   A. 12
   B. 20
   C. 24
   D. 28

12. When installing two layers of bulk or board insulation, _____.

    A. The larger R-value shall be the total R-value
    B. The R-values of each material shall be added together and divided by two (2) for a total R-value
    C. The R-values of each material shall be added together for a total R-value
    D. The R-values of each material shall be divided by their respective thicknesses and added together for a total R-value

13. When a rope is used for hoisting or supporting personnel, a safety factor of _____ must be used.

    A. 5
    B. 10
    C. 15
    D. 20

14. The MAXIMUM permitted space between rungs, cleats and steps of a portable ladders and fixed ladders shall be _____ inches.

    A. 10
    B. 12
    C. 14
    D. 16

15. Erected shoring equipment used for cast-in-place concrete operations shall be inspected _____.

    A. Prior to the placement of concrete
    B. Daily
    C. During the placement of concrete
    D. Immediately prior to, during, and after concrete placement

16. Simple slope excavations of clay loam soil that are 12 ft or less in depth and remain open short term shall have a maximum allowable slope of_____.

    A. ½ to 1
    B. ¾ to 1
    C. 1 to 1
    D. 1-1/2 to 1

17. If trusses are to be stored horizontally for more than one week, blocking should be placed beneath the stack at maximum intervals of _____ feet on-center.

    A. 10
    B. 8
    C. 6
    D. 4

18. Glass unit masonry panels shall be provided with expansion joints and shall be NOT less than_____ inches in thickness.

    A. 1/4
    B. 1/2
    C. 1/8
    D. 3/8

19. A reflective window tint material can block up to _____% of the incoming sunlight.

    A. 70
    B. 40
    C. 60
    D. 85

20. Given: Excavation is 12 feet depth and has a bottom area of 8' x 18'. Sides are sloped at ½ to 1. The volume of soil from this excavation is _____ yd³. (Select the closest answer)

    A. 185
    B. 173
    C. 204
    D. 165

21. The average R value for ¾" dead air space is _____.

    A. 0.75
    B. 0.77
    C. 0.80
    D. 0.85

22. High-density R-30 insulation batts for a cathedral ceiling are _____ inches thick.

    A. 8-1/4
    B. 9-1/4
    C. 10-1/4
    D. 10

23. The minimum area for a habitable room shall have a floor area of not less _____ square feet.

    A. 70
    B. 80
    C. 90
    D. 120

24. Air-handling units shall NOT be allowed in attics if _____.

    A. The service panel of the equipment is located within 6 ft of an attic access
    B. A device is installed to alert the owner or shut down the unit when the condensation drain is not working properly
    C. The attic access opening is of sufficient size to replace the air handler
    D. The total leakage is greater than or equal to 4 cubic feet per minute per 100 square feet

25. A 5-foot truss cannot be out of plumb more than _____ inches in its permanently set position.

    A. 1
    B. 1 1/4
    C. 1 1/2
    D. 2

26. Where preservative treated wood is used in locations where drying in service cannot readily occur, such wood shall be at a moisture content of _____ percent or less.

    A. 15
    B. 16
    C. 18
    D. 19

27. Walls required to be waterproofed shall be designed and constructed to withstand hydrostatic pressures and other lateral loads and the waterproofing shall be applied from the bottom of the wall to not less than _____ inches above the maximum elevation of the ground-water table.

    A. 10
    B. 12
    C. 14
    D. 16

28. A #7 reinforcing bar requires a _____ inch hole to be drilled in a structural steel beam.

    A. .875
    B. 1
    C. .75
    D. 1.5

29. Caulking is one of various materials generally used to seal gaps less than _____ inch (inches) in an air barrier system.

    A. 1/4
    B. 3/8
    C. 1/2
    D. 3/4

30. Guardrail screen installed between its toeboards and midrails or toprails shall consist of _____ gauge US Standard wire one-inch mesh.

    A. 18
    B. 20
    C. 22
    D. 24

31. The design of the shoring for formwork shall be prepared by_____and the erected shoring shall be inspected by an engineer qualified in structural design.

    A. A competent person
    B. A qualified designer
    C. The Architect
    D. The Engineer

32. If possible, keep sling angles greater than _____ degrees.

    A. 15
    B. 20
    C. 30
    D. 45

33. Each employee engaged in residential construction activities _____ ft or more above lower levels shall be protected by guardrail systems, safety net system, or personal fall arrest system.

    A. 4
    B. 5
    C. 6
    D. 8

34. _____ are an important area of air leakage that is often overlooked by builders.

    A. Recessed lighting fixtures
    B. Windows
    C. Doors
    D. Walls

35. The maximum framing spacing for 1/2-inch gypsum panels on ceilings when the panels are installed parallel to the framing shall be _____ inches.

    A. 16
    B. 18
    C. 20
    D. 24

36. The calculated total fire resistance for a 5" thick siliceous concrete wall faced with 5/8" Type X gypsum wall board is _____.

    A. 2 hours
    B. 2 hours and 20 minutes
    C. 2 hours and 25 minutes
    D. 2 hours and 40 minutes

37. Recordable incidents must be entered within _____ days of learning of its occurrence.

    A. 5
    B. 7
    C. 10
    D. 14

38. On exterior stud walls, adhered masonry veneer shall be installed not less than _____ inches above the earth.

    A. 2
    B. 4
    C. ½
    D. 6

39. Given: Excavation of a trench is 4 feet depth and has a bottom area of 6' x 25'. Sides are sloped at 2 to 1. The volume of soil from this excavation is _____ yd³. Select the closest answer

    A. 74
    B. 76
    C. 78
    D. 80

40. When uprights are embedded, the vertical distance from the center of the lowest cross brace in the bottom of the trench shall not exceed _____ inches.

    A. 18
    B. 30
    C. 36
    D. 42

41. The required fire-resistance rating of exterior walls with a fire separation distance from adjacent structures greater than 10 feet, shall be rated for exposure to fire from _____ of the wall.

    A. The inside
    B. The outside
    C. Both sides
    D. None of the above

42. The R-value of a 5/8" sheet of drywall is _____.

    A. .5000
    B. .5625
    C. .9000
    D. 1.200

43. _____ is NOT one of the soil sample tests that are conducted to determine quantitative as well as qualitative properties of soil.

    A. Plasticity
    B. Dry strength
    C. Thumb penetration
    D. Density test

44. Expansion joints for glass unit masonry panels shall not be less than _____ inch in thickness.

  A. ¼
  B. 3/8
  C. ½
  D. ¾

45. _____ fire extinguishers are used for electrical fires.

  A. Class A
  B. Class B
  C. Class C
  D. Class D

46. Oily rags shall be kept in _____ until removed from the worksite.

  A. A fire-resistant covered container
  B. Metal drums with cover
  C. Metal containers with cover
  D. None of the above - oily rags shall be removed from the jobsite weekly

47. Given: A utility trench is 225' long and is to be excavated to a uniform depth of 6'. The bottom of the trench must be 3' wide and the sides sloped at ½ to 1. The total volume of material to be excavated is _____ yd^3. Select the closest answer.

  A. 175
  B. 248
  C. 310
  D. 400

48. For the above referenced problem, if the soil swells 17%, the total amount of material to haul off site would be _____ yd^3. Select the closest answer.

  A. 205
  B. 290
  C. 360
  D. 468

49. Waterproofing shall be accomplished by placing a membrane not less than 6 mil polyvinyl chloride with joints lapped not less than _____ inches

  A. 2
  B. 4
  C. 6
  D. 8

50. A _____ is often indicated on a set of plans and is a point of known elevation established by a registered surveyor.

    A. Landmark
    B. Benchmark
    C. Reference point
    D. Survey mark

51. Wood framing members that are in contact with exterior foundation walls and are less than _____ inches from exposed earth shall be naturally durable or preservative-treated wood.

    A. 6
    B. 8
    C. 4
    D. 12

52. Screws for installing single layer gypsum panel products shall be spaced not more than _____ inches o.c. for ceilings or walls where framing members are 24" o.c.

    A. 6
    B. 8
    C. 12
    D. 16

53. Stair riser heights shall be _____ inches maximum and _____ inches minimum.

    A. 6 / 4
    B. 7 / 4
    C. 6 / 5
    D. 7 / 5

54. In order to eliminate scheduling conflicts, the proposed project schedule should be reviewed during the preconstruction conference _____.

    A. By the general contractor, architect and owner
    B. By all the subcontractors, major material vendors and specialty subcontractors
    C. By the local building and plan review officials
    D. By the project manager and project engineer

55. Exit access travel distance for 20 residents of an Assisted Living Facility equipped with sprinklers shall not exceed _____ feet.

    A. 75
    B. 100
    C. 200
    D. 250

56. Concrete foundation walls shall comply with the size and spacing of vertical reinforcement based on the use of reinforcement with a minimum yield strength of _____ psi.

    A. 40,000
    B. 50,000
    C. 60,000
    D. 75,000

57. Air leakage testing is not required for additions, alterations, renovations or repairs of the building envelope of existing buildings in which the new construction is less than _____ % of the building thermal envelope.

    A. 25
    B. 65
    C. 75
    D. 85

58. A stairway or ladder shall be provided at all personnel points of access where there is a break in elevation of _____ inches or more.

    A. 16
    B. 18
    C. 19
    D. 20

59. Compacted fill material 12 inches in depth or less need not comply with an approved report, provided the in-place dry density is _____ percent of the maximum dry density at optimum moisture content.

    A. Not less than 90
    B. At least 95
    C. More than 95
    D. 95

60. _____ would be the best approach to take when cooling concrete mix in hot weather.

    A. Adding more water as needed on the jobsite
    B. Extend the amount of time to be held in the mixer
    C. Tell the dispatcher to make sure aggregate is cooled before adding
    D. Adding fly ash

61. The maximum top chord temporary lateral restraint spacing for a truss span of 45ft to 60ft is _____ ft on center.

    A. 10
    B. 8
    C. 6
    D. 4

62. When W4.5 is used in the designation of welded wire reinforcement, it represents the _____ of the wire.

    A. Diameter
    B. Gauge
    C. Area
    D. Weight

63. Fireblocking shall be provided in concealed spaces between stair stringers at the _____ of the run.

    A. Middle
    B. Bottom
    C. Top
    D. Top and bottom

64. Deformed steel reinforcing bar is considered _____.

    A. Rejected
    B. Replaceable
    C. Acceptable
    D. Standard

65. No more than _____ gallons of flammable liquids shall be stored in a room outside of an approved storage cabinet.

    A. 10
    B. 20
    C. 25
    D. 60

Please see Answer Key on following page
ALH 02/15/2022

Project Management
Practice Test 3
Answer Key

CM: Florida Contractors Manual

A201, A401, A701: Various AIA documents

FBC: FL Building Code; Building/Residential/Existing Building/Energy
Conservation/ Accessibility

Walker's: Walker's Building Estimator's Reference Book

OSHA: 29 CFR 1926 OSHA Construction Industry Regulations

PPCC: Principles and Practices of Commercial Construction

DCCM: Design and Control of Concrete Mixtures

Rebar: Placing Reinforcing Bars

EEBC: Energy Efficient Building Construction in Florida

Truss: BCSI Guide to Good Practice for handling, Installing, Restraining & Bracing of
Metal Plate Connected Wood Trusses

No.	Answer	Book and page (Location)
1	C	BCSI, page 6 (TOC: "Hoisting & Placement of Truss Bundles")
2	B	FBC - Energy Conservation, sect. R403.3.1- (Index: "Duct Installation")
3	A	OSHA 1926.652 (b)(1)(i) (Index: "Excavations - Sloping and benching")
4	D	EEBC, 10th Ed. pg. 146, Table 7-5; EEBC, 9th Ed. pg. 145, Table 7-4 (Index: "Solar Heat Gain Coefficient (SHGC)")
5	D	BCSI - pg. 11 - (TOC: "Installation Tolerance")
6	B	OSHA 1926.1408 - Table A (Index: "Cranes" and "Powerlines: Cranes and Derricks")
7	C	EEBC, 10th Ed. pg. 270 Appendix II: Fingertip Facts; EEBC, 9th Ed. pg. 270 Appendix II: Fingertip Facts - Insert TAB - SEER
8	A	FBC - Building, 1209.1 - (Index: "Crawl space - Access" and "Access Openings - Crawl Space")
9	C	FBC - Energy Conservation Table R303.2.1.1 - Index: "Insulation - Installation")
10	D	FBC - Residential Table R702.3.5 - (Index: "Gypsum")
11	C	CM pg. 10-90 (Index: "Metric Conversions")
12	C	FBC - Energy Conservation sect. R303.1.1.1.2 (Index: "Insulation - Installation")
13	B	CM pg. 7-53 (Index: "Rope - Safety Factor")
14	C	OSHA 1926.1053 (a) (3) (i) (Index: "Ladders")
15	D	OSHA 1926.703 (b)(3) (Index: "Shoring - Concrete and Concrete Forms")
16	A	OSHA 1926.650 Excavations - Subpart P Appendix B Sloping and Benching - Figure B-1.1- note 1 exception (Index: "Excavations") — to identify soil as Type A (Index: "Soil Classification for Excavations")
17	A	BCSI pg. 75 (TOC: Truss Storage)
18	D	FBC - Residential sect. R607.7 (TOC: Chap 6, "Glass Unit Masonry")
19	D	EEBC, 10th Ed., pg. 150; EEBC, 9th Ed., pg. 149 (Index: "Windows")
20	D	PPCC - 9th edition page 72 / 10th edition page 77 $$\text{Volume to be excavated} = \frac{(A_1 + A_2) \times L}{2}$$ Sloped *Yr* 1 with depth of 12ft so extra 6ft on each side to be sloped back A_1 = top area = (18ft wide + 6ft one side + 6ft other side) x (8ft wide + 6ft one side + 6ft other side) = 30 ft x 20 ft = 600 ft^2

		A_2 = bottom area = 18ft x 8ft wide = 144 ft^2 L = length between the two areas or depth V = (600 ft^2 + 144 ft^2) / 2 = 372 ft^2 x 12 ft = 4464 ft^3 / 27 ft^3 in yd^3 = 165.3 yd^3
21	B	EEBC, 10th Ed. pg. 272; EEBC, 9th Ed. pg. 271 Appendix – Insert TAB - R VALUES
22	A	EEBC, 10th Ed. pg. 122 (Index: "Insulation – of Cathedral Ceilings") EEBC, 9th Ed. pg. 120 (Index: "Insulation – of Cathedral Ceilings")
23	A	FBC – Residential sect. R304.1 (TOC: Chap 3 "Building Planning: Minimum Room Areas")
24	D	FBC – Energy Conservation, sect. R403.3.6 (Index: "HVAC Systems")
25	B	BCSI, page 11 – Installation tolerances
26	D	FBC Building, 2303.1.9.2 (Index: "Wood – Moisture content")
27	B	FBC – Building, sect. 1805.3.2 (TOC: Chapter 18 – "Soils and Foundations – Dampproofing and Waterproofing")
28	A	Trade Knowledge, 7/8 = .875 Rebar – 9th edition 6-1 and 10th edition 7-1
29	A	EEBC, 10th Ed. pg. 79 (Index: "Air Barrier Systems – materials") EEBC, 9th Ed. pg. 77 (Index: "Air Barrier Systems – materials")
30	A	OSHA 1926.451 Guardrails - Scaffolds - Subpart L Appendix A Scaffold Specifications, (I)(f) (Index: "Scaffolds")
31	B	OSHA 1926.703 (b) (8) (i). (Index: "Shoring, Concrete and Concrete Forms")
32	D	CM, 2021 pg. 7-90; 2017 pg. 7-90 (Index: "Rigging – Sling Angles")
33	C	OSHA 1926.501(b)(13) (Index: "Guardrails ")
34	A	EEBC, 10th Ed. pg. 80 (TOC: "Air Leakage – see also Bypasses/Penetrations"). EEBC, 9th Ed. pg. 78 (TOC: "Air Leakage – see also Bypasses/Penetrations").
35	A	FBC – Residential, Table R702.3 (Index: "Gypsum")
36	D	FBC – Building, [Index: "Fire Resistance" - Table 722.2.1.1 and Table 722.2.1.4(2)] 5" Siliceous concrete = 2 hours 5/8" Type X gypsum = 40 minutes 2 hours and 40 minutes
37	B	CM, 2021 pg. 7-6; 2017 pg. 7-6 (Index: "OSHA – Responsibilities")
38	B	FBC – Building sect. 1405.10.1.3 (Index: "Masonry – Adhered Veneer)
39	C	Principles/Practices of Commercial Construction, 10th 77 Principles/Practices of Commercial Construction, 9th 72 Volume to be excavated = $\dfrac{(A_1 + A_2)}{2}$ x L Sloped 2:1 with depth of 4ft so extra 8ft on each side to be sloped back A_1 = top area = (6ft wide + 8ft one side + 8ft other side) x (25ft long + 8ft one side + 8ft other side) = 22ft x 41ft = 902 ft^2 A_2 = bottom area = 6ft x 25ft = 150 ft^2 L = length between the two areas or depth V = (902 ft^2 + 150 ft^2) / 2 = 526 ft^2 x 4ft = 2104 ft^3 / 27 ft^3 in yd^3 = 77.92 yd^3
40	C	OSHA 1926.652 Excavation - Subpart P Timber shoring for trenches (g)(5) Notes for all Tables (Index: "Excavations – Shoring")
41	A	FBC Building, sect 705.5 (Index: "Fire Resistance - Ratings")
42	B	EEBC, 10th Ed. pg. 271 – 5/8 x .9 = .5625 Appendix II EEBC, 9th Ed. pg. 271 – 5/8 x .9 = .5625 Appendix II
43	D	Subpart P Appendix A(d)(2) (Index: "Soil Classification")
44	B	FBC – Residential, R607.7 (TOC: "Chapter 6 – Glass Unit Masonry")

45	C	OSHA 1926.150 Table F-1 (Index: "Fire Extinguishers")
46	A	OSHA 1926.252 (e) (Index: "Disposal, Waste Materials")

47	C	Principles/Practices of Commercial Construction, 10th pg. 77 Principles/Practices of Commercial Construction, 9th pg. 72 $$\text{Volume to be excavated} = \frac{(A_i + A_2) \times D}{Z}$$ Sloped *Yr* 1 with depth of 6ft so extra 3ft on each side to be sloped back A_i = top area = (225ft + 3ft one side + 3ft other side) x (3ft + 3ft + 3ft) wide = 231 ft x 9ft = 2,079 ft^2 A_2 = bottom area = 225ft x 3ft wide = 675 ft^2 D = distance between the two areas or depth V = (2,079 ft^2 + 675 ft^2) / 2 = 1,377 ft^2 x 6ft = 8,262 ft^3 / 27 ft^3 in yd^3 = 306 yd^3
48	C	Trade Knowledge 306 yd^3 x 1.17 (swell factor) = 358 yd^3
49	C	FBC - Building sect. 1805.3.1 (TOC: "Dampproofing and Waterproofing")
50	B	PPCC pg. 30 Trade Knowledge
51	B	FBC - Building sect. 2304.12.1.2 (Index: "Wood - Contacting concrete, masonry or earth")
52	C	FBC - Residential Table R702.3.5 (Index: "Gypsum")
53	B	FBC - Building , sec 1011.5.2 (Index: "Risers, Stair - General")
54	B	CM pg. 10-64 (Index: "Scheduling - Guidelines TOC: Chap 10: "Project Schedules"-Scheduling Guidelines")
55	D	FBC - Building, sect 308.3 and Table 1017.2 (Index: "Assisted Living: Group I -1 and Index: ("Travel Distance-Exit Access")
56	C	FBC - Building, sect 1807.1.6.2(2) (Index: "Concrete - Foundation Wall")
57	D	EEBC, 10th Ed. pg. 85 Index: ("Air leakage - driving forces") EEBC, 9th Ed. pg. 83
58	C	OSHA 1926.1051(a) (Index: "Stairways see also Ladders")
59	A	FBC - Building sect. 1804.6 exception (Index: "Fill Material")
60	C	Trade Knowledge - DCCM pgs. 468 - 471
61	C	BCSI pg. 12 Temporary installation/bracing various planes and pg. 21 - Details of Truss Installation
62	C	Trade knowledge - Rebar 9th edition pp 3-1 and Rebar 10th edition pp 3-1
63	D	FBC - Building, sect. 718.2.4 (Index: "Fireblocking, Wood Stairways").
64	D	Trade knowledge - Rebar 9th edition pp 6-1 and Rebar 10th edition pp 7-1
65	C	OSHA 1926.106 (Index: "Flammable Liquids")

Made in United States
Orlando, FL
04 October 2023

37564097R00109